**Aids and Precautions
in Administering the Illinois Test
of Psycholinguistic Abilities**

DE STIJL

AIDS AND PRECAUTIONS
IN ADMINISTERING THE ILLINOIS TEST
OF PSYCHOLINGUISTIC ABILITIES

Winifred D. Kirk

UNIVERSITY OF ILLINOIS PRESS
Urbana   Chicago   London

Contents

I

Introduction

In 1961 the *Illinois Test of Psycholinguistic Abilities, Experimental Edition,* was introduced to a number of professionals interested in psychometric and educational assessment of children with learning problems. It was a limited edition of 250 handmade kits. The distribution was restricted solely to those interested in using the test experimentally to further check on its use, applicability, and reliability. The test was, as its name implied, a trial balloon. So much interest was expressed, however, and use of the test as a research and clinical tool became so widespread, that it became necessary to produce the test in much greater quantity. During the trial period we learned much about the direction the revised edition should take. From 1965 to 1968 our staff modified, extended, and thoroughly revamped much of the test, completing the revised edition in 1968.

The instructions for administering the experimental edition, though explicitly set forth in the examiner's manual for the test, left enough latitude to the examiners that there was considerable variation in administration. In the revised edition, therefore, the instructions have been rather tightly written, and the manner of administration has been narrowed considerably. These changes made possible a more consistent administration but required a more rigid and careful study of the new *Examiner's Manual* (1968). This study, we have found, has not been universally done.

At times we have found the ITPA being administered, scored, and interpreted by persons who have not studied the *Examiner's Manual* carefully, who have not sought consultation with those who know the test well, or who are not adequately trained in the administration of individual psychological tests. (The ability to administer the Binet or the WISC, for example, does not qualify an individual to administer and interpret the ITPA.) In many instances the administration of the test is being taught by persons who have not themselves been checked out or observed by adequately trained personnel. This lack of qualification, of course, has been distressing to us and leads us to question some research data based on results of ITPA testing.

The ITPA is restricted in its distribution. The publisher observes the ethical standards and practices recommended by the American Psychological Association for the publication and distribution of test materials. It is requested that use of the test be limited to those who have learned to appreciate the significance of the scientific method in test administration. They must follow the same rigor in test administration that is described in the manual for the *Stanford-Binet Intelligence Scale*. The potential examiner should read pages 15 and 16 in the *Examiner's Manual* of the ITPA and pages 46 to 59 in the *Manual, Stanford-Binet Intelligence Scale*.

We have found that people with a master's degree who have majored in psychometrics, speech and communication disorders, school counselling, or diagnostic remedial teaching and who have had some background in individual test administration can learn to administer and score the ITPA adequately. Regardless of their field of training, however, they must be conscientious enough to take the time to learn, to practice, and to be checked out by someone who has been adequately trained. The University of Illinois Press can provide trained personnel and help organize three- or five-day workshops for those who have taken the time to study the test and who have given it to children. Those interested in such a workshop should write to:

> The University of Illinois Press
> University of Illinois
> Urbana, Illinois 61801

It should be noted here that the ITPA was developed as a diagnostic tool to assess differences in abilities within individual children (intra-individual differences) in order to organize appropriate remedial programs for each child. Although the overall score of the ITPA can provide measures of intelligence comparable to an IQ and a mental age, the test was not designed as an interindividual means of categorizing, classifying, and labelling children for the purpose of placement, as were the Binet and the WISC. It is a diagnostic test and should be of most value to a diagnostic remedial specialist, just as a diagnostic reading test is best used in the hands of a competent remedial reading specialist.

The purpose of this publication is not to outline a diagnostic procedure but to clarify some of the procedures in administering the ITPA. We have found in teaching others to administer the test that there are several pitfalls and booby traps, most of which can be avoided by careful study of the *Examiner's Manual* but some of which we find need additional clarification. For this reason I have prepared this little book on aids and precautions in the administration of the ITPA.

II

Some Testing Precautions

In this section I shall try to call attention to some requirements that are often violated by inexperienced (and/or inadequate) examiners. Most of the requirements are clearly delineated in the *Examiner's Manual*, but some are easy to forget or may go unnoticed. Since many of the requirements are mentioned only in the instructions for specific tests, they are clustered here under headings which pertain to more than one subtest. The following outline of testing precautions includes some general testing precautions that should be observed as well as precautions in administering the ITPA that should be noted under the following headings:

1. Efficiency	6. Timing
2. Demonstration items	7. When to question
3. Basals	8. Recording
4. Ceilings	9. Scoring
5. Repetition of items	10. Keeping materials in good condition.

AN OUTLINE OF TESTING PRECAUTIONS

I. General testing precautions
  A. Read, learn, and *reread* instructions.
  B. Always adhere to standardized procedures.
    1. Use exact wording.
    2. Maintain accurate timing.
    3. Present materials in the prescribed manner.
    4. Follow scoring instructions rigidly.
    5. Do not depend solely on reading the printed directions, but do have them available for ready reference.
  C. Be objective.
    1. Give no indication of the correctness or incorrectness of the child's responses.
    2. Give no clues about the answer you expect; watch your verbal intonation; remember you are testing, not teaching.

D. Be natural.
   1. Be warm but impersonal.
   2. Learn to use standardized wording in a natural and informal manner.
   3. Achieve rapport and verbal give-and-take before the test begins; take a listening attitude.
E. Prepare the environment.
   1. Avoid distractions.
      a. Visual: Have the child face away from doors and windows where movement and activity are going on. Have him face away from large open spaces that have distracting pictures, colors, toys, etc. Avoid clutter.
      b. Auditory: Avoid noisy areas, other voices, etc.; test in isolation.
      c. Emotional: Avoid testing when the child is hurried, troubled, or ill.
   2. Provide optimum conditions for good performance.
      a. See that the child is in a comfortable position and has a clear view of materials.
      b. Provide a well-lit room with adequate ventilation and comfortable temperature.
      c. Avoid glaring lights, reflections from the pages, etc. Face the child away from the window if possible.
      d. Speak in a clear, audible voice at a moderate rate of speed.
      e. Maintain interest through enthusiasm, attention to the child, and smooth presentation of the material.
      f. Commend and encourage for general performance but never on specific items.
      g. Let the child know you want to see how well he can do.
II. Administering the ITPA
   A. Efficiency
      1. Provide an efficient arrangement and method of manipulating materials for
         a. Recording
         b. Viewing the manual *without its becoming a barrier between you and the child*
         c. Putting away and bringing out materials
         d. Avoiding delays and distractions for the child
      2. Make smooth transition from test to test and from item to item. You must know at each point in the test what your next presentation will be.

3. Know your materials and scoring well enough that you do not extend the test unnecessarily. Overtesting may create fatigue and/or disinterest.
   a. Know the scoring standards.
   b. Begin at the appropriate point. Children aged 6-0 and above who are not expected to be retarded should begin with Demo II.
4. Learn to handle extraneous behavior.
   a. Disregard or redirect irrelevant remarks.
   b. Minimize extraneous movements through developing interest, motivation, and task orientation. If extraneous movements do not interfere with the child's functioning, ignore them. If necessary, provide the child a positive outlet such as grasping the edges of the desk or folding his hands.
   c. Foresee fatigue and distraction.
B. Demonstration items
   1. Always *confirm or correct* the child's response to demonstration items (but *never* to test items). This cannot be emphasized too much.
   2. Repeat or expand if necessary, but always give the first and last presentations in the prescribed manner; that is, if the demonstration item has been altered to clarify or simplify it, return to the standardized wording before going on to test items. *Exception:* On the Sound Blending test, demonstration items must be given *only* as prescribed.
   3. If Demo I has been given, Demo II is presented only when so specified in the directions — namely, on the Visual Reception, Visual Association, Visual Sequential Memory, and Sound Blending tests.
   4. When beginning with Demo II, if the child fails to understand the task, revert to Demo I and proceed with Item 1.
   5. If the child persists on a wrong answer to a demonstration item, be direct; don't argue; don't hover over it.
      Examiner: Do ponies shave?
      Child: Yes.
      Examiner: No, ponies don't shave. Daddy shaves his face, but ponies do not shave, *do* they?
   6. Note unusual conditions for the following subtests:
      a. *Visual Association.* Demo I is used for all ages, but children above 6-0 begin with Item 11. Demo II is used in its

proper sequence for all children who do not reach a ceiling by Item 20.

b. *Auditory Sequential Memory*. The beginning item for children above 6-0 (Item 3) may be repeated or modified to serve as a demonstration item, in which case, of course, it is not scored. If the child fails "8-1-1" twice, it is permissible to ask him to repeat "1-1," then give him "8-1-1" again and proceed backwards with Items 2 and 1. It is also permissible, after two failures on Item 3, to go directly to Demo I. For children beginning with Demo I, Item 3 is never used as a demonstration item but is presented as a test item.

7. Never score points for demonstration items.

C. Basals

1. Note that there is no basal when beginning with Demo I and Item 1 (since the basal is that point below which success may be assumed without giving the test items).

2. When beginning with Demo II, make sure you have a basal. Go back to get the basal first when appropriate (as soon as the child makes his first failure), then go forward to get the ceiling.

3. In procuring the basal, give progressively easier items, beginning immediately below the original starting point. Note that the required number of successes may override (but never include) the intervening demonstration item; that is, any successes the child had before making his first error may be included in the required number of consecutive successes for the basal.

4. In reaching for a basal, if you are uncertain how to score an item, assume the answer to be *wrong* and keep going backward to be sure to have the prescribed number of successes after more careful consideration of the scoring.

5. Beginning examiners may find it helpful to mark the record form (before administering the test) with a bracket at Items 11, 12, and 13 or whatever basal requirements are indicated for each subtest.

6. Note precautions for the following subtests:

a. *Auditory Reception*. *Five* correct items are necessary to assume a basal. Since *three* correct items is the common requirement, beginning testers may want to bracket these five items before beginning the Auditory Reception test.

      b. *Visual Reception.* In going backward to procure a basal, be sure the child does not see the answer page before he sees the stimulus page. (Tip the book toward you to find the right page. If your Picture Book 1 does not have a tab on Item 10, double a piece of tape over the edge to help you find it more easily.)

      c. *Sequential Memory Subtests.* On both of these subtests remember that before going backward to obtain a basal, the child is given a second trial on the item on which he makes his first failure. Also note that in securing a basal, success must be achieved on the *first attempt* for an item to qualify in achieving the basal.

D. Ceilings

  1. Note the prescribed number of consecutive failures needed to assume failure on succeeding items.

  2. If testing accidentally goes beyond the ceiling, eliminate all scores beyond the legitimate ceiling. (The test is not invalidated by overreaching the ceiling, but testing time is unnecessarily extended and the child may become fatigued and/or discouraged.)

  3. In reaching for a ceiling, if you are uncertain how an item should be scored, assume the answer to be *correct* and continue testing to be sure to have the prescribed number of failures after more careful consideration of the scoring.

  4. On the Auditory Reception test be careful to count correctly to find three errors within seven (or fewer) consecutive items. (When the child makes his first mistake, some examiners like to count six more items and put a mark there; when two more mistakes are made before the mark is reached, they stop testing.)

E. Repetition of items

  1. Repetition of spoken material is permissible on tests if the child requests it, except, of course, on both Sequential Memory subtests and the Sound Blending test.

  2. Test items are never repeated after the child has responded (unless it is absolutely clear he has misunderstood the item — for example, if the school bell rang in the middle of the item presentation and he gave a wild or irrelevant answer).

  3. If the child says, "I don't know," or if he asks your opinion, it is permissible (with the following exceptions in points

E.4, E.5, and E.6) to say, "What do you think?" or "Which one do you think it might be?" and repeat the item.

4. *One repetition only* is permissible on the Auditory Closure test.

5. On the Auditory Association test, if the child completes an opposite analogy by merely negating the initial statement (for example, "A rabbit is fast; a turtle is not fast") say "No" and repeat the item (only once per item, for not more than two items). These repetitions should be clearly indicated on the record form.

6. On the Grammatic Closure test a second trial is given only when the child fails to use some form of the anticipated response (see Section V). This repetition may be done only once per item but for as many items as necessary. Never repeat the item when the child uses a wrong form of the anticipated response.

F. Timing

1. Rate of the examiner's presentation of oral material

   a. In general, your rate of speech must be natural and easy to understand. Examiners who naturally speak very fast must guard against presenting test items too rapidly or speaking too fast. On the other hand, unnaturally slow speech must be avoided.

   On the Auditory Association test you are not testing the child's ability to grasp the verbal material but his ability to deal with it in recognizing relationships. You do not want failure on this test to be caused by failure to understand the material. (The verbal receptive content of this subtest, it should be remembered, is geared about two years below the cognitive ability to grasp relationships. The item "A block is square; a ball is ————" taxes auditory reception much less than "A cube is square; a sphere is ————.") The material for the Auditory Association test should be presented at a natural but relaxed rate, not an abnormally slow one.

   b. There are two subtests (Auditory Sequential Memory and Sound Blending) that require a specific rate of presentation at one-half second intervals. The digits in the Auditory Sequential Memory test should be timed exactly. (Try to internalize the timing by practicing with a stopwatch, or better still, with a metronome set at 120 beats per minute.) The separate sounds in the Sound Blending test should also approach the one-half-second intervals. These phonic elements should be spoken just as they are *heard* in the word, not as they look on paper.

The phonic elements of the Sound Blending test should be presented at half-second intervals, with a distinct break between sounds. Some examiners do not have the knack of presenting this test. If you feel uncertain about your ability in this area you should be checked by an expert. Also listen over and over to the record in the ITPA kit until you can duplicate each word (see Section IV). Never present this test by way of a tape recording.

2. Timing of the exposure of visual materials

   a. On the Visual Reception test it is not necessary to use a stopwatch. Learn to recognize a three-second interval (which is about the time necessary to reach for and turn page 2 of the item). Check yourself occasionally with a stopwatch.

   b. On the Visual Sequential Memory test timing must be exact. Use a stopwatch if at all possible; otherwise, use a sweep-second-hand watch. The stopwatch may be laid on the table and left in continuous operation, requiring only a glance to assure the sweep-second timing.

   The five-second timing begins as you finish the instructions. But remember that the total time that the child is looking at the sequence of figures includes the time you are giving instructions; therefore, the wording must be followed exactly and must be coordinated with the exposure of the sequence in the booklet. Do not expose the sequence and then delay your instructions. Give the instructions as you expose the sequence and speak at a moderate speed. Do not rush; do not delay.

   c. On the Visual Closure subtest a stopwatch or sweep-second-hand watch is essential. Open the strip for each item with the words "Begin here. Point to each one," and begin your timing immediately.

   d. On the Verbal Expression subtest timing need not be exact, but you should be aware of the time elapsed. The one-minute time suggested has some latitude and depends on how the child is responding. If he is still producing *relevant, discrete,* and *factual* responses, do not stop him. On the other hand, it is not necessary to push a taciturn child beyond his ability to produce responses. He should, however, be stimulated by attentive encouragement during a reasonable time period. "Tell me more about it" or "Tell me something else" may be used as verbal encouragement a maximum of five times. Therefore, you should indicate these on the record form, perhaps with an *E* inserted between the child's responses.

G. When to question
  1. Question when necessary to clarify the meaning of the child's answer (see the *Examiner's Manual*).
  2. Question when necessary to understand the child's speech (use sparingly).
  3. Too little questioning may deprive the child of credit; too much questioning wastes time and sometimes invalidates responses because the child thinks his original response was wrong.
  4. Question when the child chooses more than one answer. Ask, "Which one do you think it might be?"
H. Recording
  1. Record responses immediately.
  2. Record verbatim when any doubt about scoring exists.
  3. Record in such a manner that another person can score the test.
  4. Be sensitive to the child's awareness of your recording. Many children show surprising facility in reading upside down and in interpreting scoring codes. On the Auditory Sequential Memory test it is especially important to at least screen the digit sequences with your finger. It is a good idea to attach the record form to a clipboard so it can be tilted away from the child or used in your lap.
  5. On the Auditory Association subtest be sure to indicate where the child was given a second trial because he negated the statement instead of giving the opposite. Only two items may be thus repeated (see *Examiner's Manual* page 35).
  6. As a precaution against losing your place in reading the items (as on the Auditory Reception and Auditory Association tests) a 3 by 5 card may be moved down the page as you progress from item to item.
  7. In recording responses during a test, it is helpful to keep

the pencil on the item just marked while presenting the next item. It is very easy, when your eyes move away from the record form, to record a response in the wrong place.

8. Be sure to record all identifying information.

    a. Always give the necessary information on the face sheet, especially the names of the child and the examiner and the date or dates of the test.

    b. Always write "Practice Test" across the face sheet if the test administered is not a bona fide test by an experienced examiner.

    c. Always put the child's name and the date on the visual closure picture strips and clip all five of them together. If the strips are not labeled and become separated from the record form the test may be confused with another child's data.

I. Scoring

1. It is essential that an examiner know the scoring standards well. This requirement applies particularly to the understanding of the *intent* of each subtest. On both the Manual Expression subtest and the Verbal Expression subtest the administration is dependent on an adequate knowledge of the scoring.

2. It must be remembered that the scoring standards are just what the label states: they are "standards" for scoring rather than all-inclusive right-or-wrong answers. It is often necessary to evaluate equivalent responses in the light of other responses listed in the scoring standards, since not all possible responses could be included.

3. Many arbitrary decisions had to be made in establishing the scoring standards in order to maintain internal consistency. Since these were the standards used in scoring the normative sample, they must, of course, be followed explicitly.

4. A beginning examiner should check all answers with the *Examiner's Manual* in order to verify any doubtful responses.

5. During the administration of such tests as Auditory Association, Grammatic Closure, and especially Manual Expression, the scoring standards must be readily available. On the Manual Expression test it is difficult, if not impossible, to recheck the scoring, since the action must be scored on the spot. On this test it is important to keep your eyes on the child until he has finished each item. Then the item can be

scored. It is easy to miss an important gesture while you are glancing at the scoring sheet.

6. On the Visual Closure test be sure to use the tissue overlays until you are certain which incomplete figures are scored.

7. Self-corrections are accepted and scored if they are made spontaneously during the presentation of the item in question or the item immediately following. (Sometimes it is necessary to verify the child's intent.)

8. Demonstration items are *never* scored. It is wise, however, to record the responses to demonstration items.

9. Every step in the scoring process should be rechecked.

10. In obtaining scores from Tables 1 and 2 of *Examiner's Manual* Appendix A, care must be taken in finding the correct column and row. Speed and accuracy are improved by using a 3 by 5 card with a small arrow or other mark at the center of the top edge. The arrow can be used to maintain the right column and the top edge of the card to find the row.

11. All figures and calculations should be double-checked. The chronological age (figured to the nearest month), the number of correct items, additions, and arithmetic calculations — all should be double-checked.

J. Keeping materials in good condition

1. Whenever any of the materials presented to the child become marked or defaced in any way that might influence the child's response, they should be replaced.

2. If repeated pointing with dirty fingers has smeared certain responses on the visual subtests, the pages in the picture books can be washed with soap and water and a damp cloth, though care should be used to dry them as well as possible and flatten them out while they are still damp.

3. In some subtests, such as Visual Reception, Visual Association, and Grammatic Closure, the examiner must point to the pictures in the picture book. In doing so, be sure not to mark the page. Use the back end of your pen or pencil.

4. If any materials are lost or damaged, they should be replaced by objects *identical to the original*. For replacements, write to the University of Illinois Press. Likewise, if any kits contain imperfect items (such as the chips for the Visual Sequential Memory test) these items should be exchanged for perfect ones.

5. The envelope for the Verbal Expression test often becomes marked or wrinkled. You should carry a supply of fresh envelopes so that a fresh one may be presented to the child. It is necessary that the substitute envelope be identical, with the same color, size, areas of glue, and the like.

III

Precautions in Administering the Visual Sequential Memory Subtest

On the following pages are presented some suggestions and some precautions for the Visual Sequential Memory subtest, which sometimes presents pitfalls if procedure is not studied carefully. It is hoped that the precautions presented here will stimulate rather than replace a more careful study of the ITPA *Examiner's Manual.*

This test requires more practice than do the other subtests for the examiner to achieve a smooth administration technique. I suggest that the student practice the words and movements with his book open as he pretends he has a subject across from him. It is sometimes easier to memorize the words first and then incorporate the movements. Each step in the procedure should be carefully matched with the directions in the *Manual.* After some facility has been achieved, the examiner should administer the test to an adult, who will follow the procedure in the *Manual* as the practice test is being administered.

The potential examiner may also gain from more than one viewing of that part of the 16-mm *Film Demonstration of the Revised ITPA* (Kirk and Kirk, 1969) which pertains to the Visual Sequential Memory subtest.

The directions for administration of this subtest are presented here in a somewhat different format from that of the directions presented in the *Examiner's Manual.* The words and movements, however, are the same. Column 1 presents only the action followed by the examiner, Column 2 presents the words used, and Column 3 presents certain precautions to be observed and should answer some of the questions which arise during the initial phases of learning the test.

These directions and precautions should be used in conjunction with Appendix D, which presents a sequence of photographs illustrating the step-by-step procedure in administering this subtest.

DEMONSTRATION:

| Ss below 6-0 begin with Demo I | Ss 6-0 and above begin with Demo II |

ACTION

E places the 17 chips on the table (out of S's reach, but not necessarily out of his sight).

Then, placing the appropriate chips in front of S and placing the tray between S and the chips, E says,

WORDS

SEE THESE?

PRECAUTIONS

The tray must be placed *between* the child and the chips. The open edge of the tray should be *toward* you so that you will be able to slide the chips out toward yourself.

Do not put the tray out first and then begin to fumble with the chips and booklet. You can avoid much fumbling if the booklet is opened to the correct page and then placed face down in front of you while you select the appropriate chips and place them *and* the tray in front of the child almost simultaneously.

E opens the test booklet to the appropriate sequence in such a manner as to cover the chips and the tray, saying

WE'RE GOING TO MAKE THIS ...

Pause for a few seconds to let the child look at the sequence.

Be sure *both* the tray and the chips are covered by the booklet. The booklet should lie flat.

E closes the booklet and picks up the first chip (like the one on S's left in the booklet). As he places it in the tray, he says:

... RIGHT HERE.

As you close the booklet, expose the tray and reach for the first chip.

Do *not* point to the tray. Exposing the tray and placing the first chip shows the child what you mean by "right here."

Be sure to hide the sequence in the booklet.

As E places the chips on the tray from S's left to right in the same sequence and orientation as the stimulus, he says:

THIS ONE HERE AND THIS ONE HERE, etc.

As you reach for each succeeding chip say, "This one ..."; as you place it say, "... here."

On Demo II, be sure to place the slash marks in the same direction as they are in the booklet (slash mark pointing to the corner of the tray).

ACTION

Then re-exposing the sequence in the booklet and holding it adjacent to and parallel to the tray, E shows the likeness, saying,

Closing the booklet momentarily, E slides the chips from the tray (toward himself) and mixes them.

E then re-exposes the sequence in the booklet, covering tray and chips, and says,

WORDS

SEE? THIS ONE . . . (pointing to the first figure in the booklet)

. . . HERE . . . (pointing to the corresponding chip on the tray)

. . . AND THIS ONE . . . (pointing to the second figure in the booklet)

. . . HERE (pointing to the corresponding chip on the tray).

NOW LOOK AGAIN SO *YOU* CAN MAKE IT.

PRECAUTIONS

Note that you point first to the figure in the booklet, then to the tray.

Note also that the long side of the booklet is adjacent to the long side of the tray so that each chip is directly below its corresponding figure as the child sees it.

Be sure to twist the chips around so that they are not left in the same relationship as in the picture sequence.

The chips need not be in a straight line or in any particular attitude (up/down or right/left orientation), but all should be plainly visible and none overlapping.

Five seconds after finishing the instructions, E closes the booklet, saying,

THIS ONE HERE AND THIS ONE HERE, etc. (pointing to each figure in turn from S's left to right).

After S arranges the chips, E re-exposes the sequence in the booklet, allowing direct comparison, and says,

YOU DO IT. MAKE IT HERE (pointing to tray).

This is the only situation in which you need to point to the tray.

E points from each figure in the booklet to its correct position on the tray (rearranging the chips if necessary) and says,

YES (NO), IT WAS LIKE THIS.

"YES" and "NO" are alternatives, depending on whether the child has been successful or not.

THIS ONE (in the booklet)
HERE (on the tray)
AND THIS ONE (in booklet)
HERE (on tray), etc.

If the child reproduces the wrong sequence of chips, it is necessary to point first to the first figure in the booklet (**THIS ONE**), then find the corresponding chip and put it in place as you say, **"HERE"** (or point to it if it is in its correct position); then do the same with the next figure in the booklet, etc., rearranging the chips so they look like the sequence in the booklet.

If the child reproduces the correct sequence but with one or more of the

PRECAUTIONS

chips in the wrong attitude (for example, with the slash going in the wrong direction), you should confirm the child's correct placement but shift the direction of the slash so that the finished product looks like the sequence in the booklet.

(It should be noted here that *on no test item* can such a reorientation be done; nor should the child be penalized for a twisted chip. It is done on the *demonstration item only*, since this is the only time a direct comparison is made. The child should see that the arrangement on the tray looks like the sequence in the booklet.)

No second trial is given if only the attitude of the chip was changed.

WORDS

LOOK AGAIN SO YOU CAN MAKE IT.

THIS ONE HERE AND THIS ONE HERE, etc.

ACTION

If S's arrangement was not correct, he is given a second trial. Sliding the chips from the tray and mixing them, E re-exposes the sequence as before and says,

(pointing to each figure from S's left to right in turn),

When S is correct on either trial, E confirms his success as above and proceeds with the test items.

YES, IT WAS LIKE THIS. THIS ONE (in booklet) HERE (on tray) AND THIS ONE (in booklet) HERE, etc.

Confirmation on demonstration items should always be positive and enthusiastic.

If S is still unsuccessful after two trials, E gives such tutelage as necessary. For Ss who began with Demo II, E may have to administer Demo I and proceed as for Ss 4-0 to 6-0.

For Ss unable to perform successfully on Demo I, E may use the practice exercises in the front of the booklet to familiarize S with reproducing a single figure. S is presented with two chips, the circle and the square, and is asked to reproduce the practice exercises one at a time. E then returns to Demo I followed by Item 1 and proceeds item by item with no sampling.

If the child is successful on either the first or second trial of Demo I, proceed to the appropriate test item.

TEST:

Ss below 4-0 begin with Item 1 and proceed item by item.	Ss 4-0 to 6-0 begin with Item 2 and follow *Sampling Procedure.*

Ss 6-0 and above begin with Item 5 and follow *Sampling Procedure.*

ACTION

For all Ss, E lays out the appropriate chips and covers them *and* the tray with the test booklet open to the corresponding sequence card, saying,

For 2- and 3-figure sequences, E says,

For sequences with 4 or more figures, E says,

Five seconds after finishing the instructions, E closes the booklet, saying,

WORDS

NOW LOOK AT THIS ONE.

THIS ONE HERE AND THIS ONE HERE, etc.

TAKE A GOOD LOOK SO YOU CAN MAKE IT.

YOU MAKE IT.

PRECAUTIONS

To avoid distraction and direct the child's attention to the upcoming sequence, both the chips and the tray must be covered by the booklet (lying flat).

This distinction in wording must be made at this point since it becomes too cumbersome to continue pointing out the separate chips when there are more than three. For young children, pointing was necessary to hold their attention.

Timing must be exact. It must begin as

the directions are completed and end as the booklet is closed. Use a stopwatch if at all possible.

If S is unsuccessful, E slides the chips out of the tray, mixes them, and says,

NOT QUITE.

This should be said in an encouraging but matter-of-fact manner.

Then re-exposing the sequence, E repeats the above administration.

NOW LOOK AGAIN. THIS ONE HERE AND THIS ONE HERE AND THIS ONE HERE (or NOW LOOK AGAIN. TAKE A GOOD LOOK SO YOU CAN MAKE IT).

The original form of presentation should be repeated, identifying the sequence by the appropriate words.

If S is unsuccessful on this second trial, E proceeds to the next appropriate item without further comment.

Keep pleasant. Give no indication as to success or failure.

If the child persists in asking if he is right, give a noncommittal response or encourage his general behavior.

If S is successful on any trial, E does not confirm or re-expose the sequence but proceeds to the next appropriate item (see Sampling Procedure, *Examiner's Manual* page 27).

You *never* confirm or correct the response to a test item; nor does the child ever receive more than two trials on an item. He is given the second trial only if he fails on the first trial.

After the test is finished, you can save time by quickly getting the chips out of sight and proceeding directly to the Auditory Association test. Before returning the chips to their plastic bag, be sure to make sure all seventeen of them are there.

The chart to be used for the upcoming sequence is the one on the facing page of the sequence the child is working on. This allows you to prepare for the next sequence while the child is working. For

Use of the notations on the back of each sequence card (from Examiner's Manual page 30): Only those chips needed in a given sequence are available to S. As the new figures are included in the sequences, corresponding chips are added and unneeded ones removed according to notations on the back of each sequence card, as listed below:

1. The bottom notations are to be used when the items are presented consecutively.

2. The center notations are to be used when sampling.

example, the notations facing sequence number 8 are:

	NEXT ITEM	ADD	REMOVE
OBTAINING BASAL	7	/	⌀
SAMPLING	12	丩 ‡	◇
OBTAINING CEILING	9	⚹	◈

This means that: (1) if sampling has been discontinued or is not appropriate, the next item to be presented is Item 9; the ⚹ will be added and the ◇ will be removed; (2) if, during sampling, the child succeeds on Item 8, the next item to be presented is Item 12; the 丩 and ‡ will be added and the ◇ will be removed; and (3) if the child fails Item 8 and has not yet acquired a basal, the next item to be presented is Item 7; the slash mark will be needed, and the ⌀ will be removed.

3. The top notations are to be used when proceeding backwards to find a basal level.

While S is working on a given sequence, E notes which chips are to be added or taken away for the upcoming sequence.

When S finishes an item, the new chips to be added are placed on the table before the other chips are slid out of the tray. Then the chips not needed are removed and the next item is presented (i.e., first add new chips; then slide

ACTION

chips from tray; then remove unneeded chips). *Care should be taken to see that the chips to be used are not laid out in the prescribed sequence, but scattered at random.*

(From page 27 of the *Examiner's Manual*) A *Sampling Procedure* is used with Ss 4-0 and above, as follows:

1. E administers only starred items until S fails on the first trial of any starred *test* item. (Demo II is always given but not scored.)

2. When such a failure occurs, E presents the second trial of that item and discontinues sampling.

3. E then proceeds backward through any unadministered test items until 3 *consecutively listed* (not necessarily consecutively presented) test items (not

PRECAUTIONS

You will find it most efficient to establish the habit of first presenting the new chips needed, then sliding the old chips out of the tray, then removing the ones not needed for the next sequence. *Put, Dump, Take.*

During the sampling procedure, if the child succeeds only on the second trial of a sampling item and then (during backward progression) fails two consecutive items on both trials each, this is considered a *false ceiling* and does not eliminate the need to find a *true ceiling* above the one point of credit already earned on the more difficult item. After the basal has been obtained, the examiner returns to the more difficult items

Demo II) have been passed on the first trial each.

4. E then returns to the point where the first failure occurred in sampling and [when necessary] continues testing until 2 *consecutively listed* test items have been failed on both trials each. *These 2 consecutive items failed must be beyond any successes achieved in the Sampling Procedure.*

and proceeds until a *true ceiling* has been obtained above any credit already earned.

Failure on both trials of a sampling item, of course, may be counted in the two failures necessary to determine the ceiling.

IV

Precautions in Administering and Scoring the Verbal Expression Subtest

The scoring and administration of this subtest must be discussed together, since adequate administration is dependent on your proficiency in evaluating individual responses. It is extremely necessary, for example, to know when and how to question the child's ambiguous responses. You must know when credit is specifically denied (for example, for the "top" of the button) and when a response should be questioned (for example, for "this part here"). It is also necessary to record the child's responses verbatim so that later, when you score the test, the child's remarks will appear in context. For inexperienced examiners a tape recorder may be helpful, but continued use of this device during legitimate tests is inadvisable, since it changes the presentation from that used during standardization. Some children may be intimidated by the device, and others may be stimulated and may become dramatic. Temporary use of the tape recorder will show the examiner how easy it is to miss some responses.

Scoring techniques on this test do take considerable study and are not acquired overnight. Even after you become adept at scoring, many responses take careful evaluation and a rereading of the requisites for scoring. In learning to score this test, you should first carefully read the scoring instructions in the *Examiner's Manual* and then try your hand at scoring the protocols presented on *Manual* pages 59–60 and in *Manual* Appendix B (pages 129–36).

DIFFICULTIES IN SCORING THE VERBAL EXPRESSION SUBTEST

The following are among the points of difficulty often encountered in learning to score this subtest adequately.

1. It is necessary to have a firm understanding of what this subtest purports to assess. It must be remembered that it attempts to evaluate not only the child's ability to put his ideas into words, but also his attempt to express the idea. It takes into account the number of dis-

crete, relevant, and factual ideas the child can express, but it does not reflect the elegance of expression or grammatical propriety.

2. It is necessary to develop a thorough understanding of the ten categories under which credit is allowed. It will be found that these ten categories are mutually exclusive and collectively exhaustive. They provide a schema by which scoring is made easier, since they narrow and define the limits within which credit is allowed.

3. It is necessary to have a thorough understanding of when to question a child's response. This understanding involves a knowledge of the scoring conventions described on *Examiner's Manual* pages 55 to 58. As this knowledge becomes more internalized, the ability to know when to have the child clarify his remark becomes more automatic. Too much questioning, of course, may penalize the child by involving new concepts which later might have been expressed spontaneously but which cannot be given credit following a question for further elaboration. On the other hand, too little questioning may deny the child credit for a legitimate concept that is implied but not expressed.

4. It is necessary to develop a feeling for grammar, as such. Although the syntax and inflections of words are not important in scoring this subtest, the logic of grammar is important in knowing what the child is referring to and in knowing when to question. It is necessary,
$$4$$
for example, to clarify whether the child is saying "This is paper"
$$0$$
(composition) or "This is a paper" (used as a label and denied credit)
$$5 \quad 10$$
or "You put paper in it" (a commonly associated object, given credit
$$5$$
in Category 10) ; to know the difference between "This is a bouncing
$$1 \qquad\qquad\qquad 10 \quad 1$$
ball" (Category 5) and "This is a jack ball" (Category 10 denoting a ball associated with the game of jacks) ; or to know how to differen-
$$1 \qquad\qquad\qquad\qquad\qquad 10$$
tiate "It is a toy" (a classification label) and "Put it with the toys" (an associated object).

5. Perhaps of most importance, it is necessary to avoid overconfidence. Always maintain a skeptical attitude toward your initial impression; many responses are not what they appear at first glance. For
$$5$$
example, "The place where you sew through" sounds like a good description of a major part of the button. However, this would get credit under the function, *sew*, rather than under the major part,

since no definitive substantive has been given. Never wean yourself from the scoring standards and the scoring instructions. This is an important point because some arbitrary decisions had to be made in the categories developing the schema — for example, the arbitrary limitations in Labels and Major Parts. As noted on *Examiner's Manual* pages 52–53, the examiner must refer to the scoring standards to determine which major parts are creditable.

RÉSUMÉS OF SCORING INSTRUCTIONS

Because the scoring instructions have been given in such detail, Tables 1 and 2 are provided as résumés of the scoring instructions. These résumés should not be relied upon exclusively without a careful reading and frequent reference to the more complete instructions on *Examiner's Manual* pages 51 through 58, from which the résumés have been extracted. It will really be more instructional to make your own résumé by careful study of the scoring instructions.

The scoring standards for each item should also be studied carefully. Again, it must be remembered that the scoring standards are exactly what the term implies: they are standards by which the examiner may evaluate other responses. They are *not* the only responses that receive or that are denied credit. Note that it is often necessary to extrapolate from one category to another and from one item to another in order to be consistent in crediting responses.

It should also be pointed out that you may not always agree with the decisions made in the scoring standards. Some arbitrary decisions had to be made during the construction of the test in order to maintain consistency from item to item and from category to category. These decisions were often influenced by the frequency with which certain responses were made by the children in the normative sample and the ages of the children so responding. Even if you think a wrong decision has been made it is wise to follow the scoring standards, since those are the decisions on which the norms were obtained. You will find such disagreements in few if any responses if the scoring instructions and sample protocols have been carefully studied.

SOME DIFFICULT SCORING DECISIONS

The responses listed in Table 3 are presented to help you evaluate your own scoring on some of the more subtle points. Many of the examples are marginal in character, but the scoring of others will

TABLE 1. RÉSUMÉ OF CATEGORIES OF CREDITABLE RESPONSES FOR VERBAL EXPRESSION
(Pages 51–54 of the ITPA *Examiner's Manual*)

General Requirements for Credit	The child's response must be: Relevant, Discrete, Factual
Category 1 LABEL	Only one point May be credited even following Q (see *Examiner's Manual*, p. 57), May be credited in an otherwise irrelevant remark (see *Examiner's Manual*, p. 55), May be imbedded in another response. Additional point may be given for classification.
Category 2 COLOR	Credit any color, but only one for object as a whole. Additional point may be given for color of major part. Credit any reference to color (even "What color is that?").
Category 3 SHAPE	Give credit if correct within class of shapes (for example, "square" for "cube"). Credit must be for specific shape or geometric term ("Shaped $\frac{3}{}$ like a circle," not "Shaped like a $\frac{9}{}$ box"). Multiple credit is given if reference is made to different *parts* or *dimensions*.
Category 4 COMPOSITION	Only one point for object as a whole. Additional points for major parts. Accept "educated guess" (see scoring standards).
Category 5 FUNCTION	Multiple points of credit. One point for each action or function which is specific to and descriptive of the item. These are usually verbs or derived from verbs.
Category 6 MAJOR PARTS	All acceptable major parts are listed in the scoring standards. One point for each. Must be a noun label (or synonym). Description of a major part (that is, by function or shape or comparison) is not credited here but may be credited under the other category.
Category 7 NUMEROSITY	Credit numerials referring to any dimension, major part, and/or the object itself. Only one point for any one dimension, part, or item. Give credit if numeral is within one-half to twice the actual number.
Category 8 OTHER PHYSICAL CHARACTERISTICS	Credit reference to size, texture, smell, weight, density, brightness, etc. Credit reference to method of construction. Use proper questioning when response is ambiguous.

TABLE 1. (Continued)

General Requirements for Credit	The child's response must be: Relevant, Discrete, Factual
Category 9 COMPARISON	Credit direct comparisons ("It is like a _____"). Credit reference to make-believe uses. Credit responses stating what the item could be if certain changes were made. Give additional credit for any stated concept by which the $\frac{3}{9}$ comparison is made (for example, "It is round like an orange").
Category 10 PERSON, PLACE OR THING	Must be a noun. Must be specific to and frequently associated with the particular item.

TABLE 2. RÉSUMÉ OF "OTHER SCORING CONVENTIONS"
(Pages 54–58 of the ITPA *Examiner's Manual*)

I. Noncreditable Responses	These are responses that are not (A) relevant, (B) discrete, and (C) approximately factual. They include new and otherwise creditable responses which follow questioning by the examiner; i.e., only in the category of Label are such responses given credit.
A. Responses That Are Not Relevant	Accidental details, emotional and personal reactions, references to extraneous objects (not the object at hand), motor gestures, universal statements (which refer to a large number of objects) — these do not receive credit. *Note:* Be alert to creditable responses which may be imbedded in an otherwise noncreditable statement. *Note:* An acceptable label receives credit even when referring to an object not at hand.
B. Responses That Are Not Discrete (Redundant Responses)	Repetitive responses (the same term used in the *same* category) do not receive a second point. Other redundant responses (synonyms and closely related concepts) do not receive a second point if they refer to the same object or part. *Note:* Additional credit may be given for a synonym (but not an identical word) only if it refers to different parts or functions.

TABLE 2. (Continued)

C. Responses Lacking Approximate Factuality	Mislabelling (see scoring standards, also *Examiner's Manual* page 56). Misinformed responses (clearly contrary to fact).
II. Conditionally Creditable Responses (Ambiguous Responses)	These responses must be clarified by proper questions (see *Examiner's Manual* page 57). No credit is given for new concepts introduced during clarification, but clarified terms in the original response may be credited. *Note:* For Label (only) credit is given if it is introduced during clarification of another response.
A. Indefinite Responses	Credit is given only if the remarks following Q explain the original term adequately.
B. Too Specific Responses	Do not give credit if the reference is to some fact not commonly shared by others unless adequately explained.
C. Relative Terms	A term usually not acceptable may sometimes receive credit after questioning if it is used relatively (the ball is bigger than a marble; the button is not shiny like a mirror).
D. Possibly Misinformed Responses	These should be questioned. Do not project your own interpretation into what the child means. Do not deny credit when he has a creditable interpretation that you may not have been aware of.
III. Other Creditable Responses A. Negative Responses	Give credit if they are factual and not bizarre and if they conform to other requirements.
B. Interrogative Responses	Creditable responses contained in a question are given credit if they are not negated in response to "What do you think?"
IV. Borderline Responses	Give credit only if careful study of the scoring instructions and scoring standards does not justify denial of credit. (This is not a substitute for careful study of the scoring requirements.)

TABLE 3. INDEX TO SOME SCORING DECISIONS

Child's Response	Category	Example	Page
Item: Ball			
It's big. [Q] Real big like a ball.	1	2	40
Play ball.	10	1	59
Play baseball.	10	2	60
It's a round head. [Q] Like a puppet.	9	6	58
It's a blue ball.	2	1	43
Shaped like a ball.	3	1	44
It's rubber. . . . It's something like plastic.	4	1	45
The dog chews it.	5	1	46
They bust. [Q] Get a nail and stick it in it and it gets flat.	5	2	46
It's green. . . . It's red.	2	4	43
Claydough. [Q] Made out of claydough.	4	7	46
There is a round thing around the ball. [Q] (repeated same)	3	5	44
Can't hear nothing in it.	5	3	47
It's a bouncing ball.	5	4	47
It's one inch across.	8	5	57
It's about one inch.	7	3	55
You can bowl with it.	5	18	50
My brother has a great big ball.	1	10	42
People and animals play with it.	10	3	60
When you throw it on the roof, the dog can't get it.	10	4	60
It's a baseball.	1	7	41
It's a ball thing.	1	7	41
Can play ping-pong with it.	5	19	51
Shaped like a circle.	3	1	44
Item: Block			
Shaped like a block.	1	1	40
What color is it?	2	2	43
Made out of brick.	4	2	45
Can turn it over and it will stay in place.	5	5	47
It is one inch high.	8	5	57
It is sharp on one corner.	7	1	55
This one is green.	7	1	55
For a light on the top of a fire engine.	9	4	58
Hide it in the playroom.	5	6	47
Has ten flat places. [Q] Ten flat parts.	6	2	51
Has ten flat places. [Q] Ten squares.	6	2	51
Has ten flat places. [Q] Ten square parts.	6	2	51
It's fat.	8	1	56
It's about one inch high and one inch wide.	8	5	57
At bedtime you can hide the block somewhere in your toys.	10	5	60

TABLE 3. (Continued)

Child's Response	Category	Example	Page
It's about one inch.	7	3	55
Flat on all ends.	6	4	52
It's real sharp here. [Q] (pointed)	6	5	52
It's one by one by one.	7	3	55
It's about one inch high and one inch wide.	8	5	57
The corners are round.	3	4	44
It's made out of hard stuff. [Q] Hard stuff like wood.	4	6	46
It's made out of hard stuff. [Q] It's real hard.	4	6	46
It has six sharp corners but these two are round.	7	4	56
A square head. [Q] Can hammer it square.	9	5	58
Each side is the same size.	8	3	56
It doesn't bounce.	5	3	47
It's soft. [Q] Smooth when you rub it.	8	4	57

Item: Envelope

Child's Response	Category	Example	Page
It's an envelope. . . . You use this stationery to write on.	1	6	41
It is yellow . . . white. [Q] The glue is yellow and the paper is white.	2	5	44
It's a paper for putting letters in.	4	4	45
It's to not let the letter fall out. [Q] Lick it right here and it sticks.	5	7	48
It looks like a house with this up. [Q] Hold the flap up and it looks like a house.	6	6	52
It's four inches by six inches.	7	3	55
It's got four corners and a thing like a tent. [Q] A piece that folds over.	6	8	53
Can make a house. [Q] With this up.	9	12	59
Can make a plane. [Q] You fold it.	9	12	59
Can make paper dolls. [Q] Cut them out with scissors.	9	12	59
It's a letter.	1	8	41
It's paper . . . made out of wood.	4	3	45
To put a valentine there. [Q] (No response)	5	8	48
Can squash it.	5	10	48
It has a hole. [Q] An open place here.	6	10	53
It's four by six.	7	3	55
It's about six inches long. It could be ten inches long.	8	5	57
It's mail. . . . It comes in the mail. . . . You can mail it.	1	9	42
It's two inches wide and four inches long.	8	5	57
Can put a letter in it. . . . It holds money.	5	11	48

TABLE 3. (Continued)

Child's Response	Category	Example	Page
You read it.	5	12	49
Write a letter to your grandma.	5	17	50
It's wrinkled.	8	7	57
It's real sharp here. [Q] (pointed)	8	6	52
Item: Button			
Some buttons have four holes.	1	11	42
My buttons have four holes.	1	11	42
It's white. . . . It's clear.	2	3	43
It's a fat button. [Q] It's round.	8	1	56
It's a fat button. [Q] It's big.	8	1	56
It's a fat button. [Q] It's real fat.	8	1	56
Fastens clothes together. . . . If it comes loose, you fasten it back on.	5	13	49
It's got a funny thing. [Q] The glass button's got a bump around it.	6	7	53
It's got two holes in the center and another hole almost like a triangle, something like a boat.	6	11	54
It's got a little thing like a little football. [Q] This.	6	9	53
Put it on your shirt or use it to button up your coat.	10	7	61
It's for to button.	5	20	51
It's round on the top and flat on the bottom.	6	13	55
You can look through it with one eye.	7	2	55
It has a little place to sew through. [Q] See, here?	6	3	51
It's round and it has two little round holes.	6	12	54
You can break it.	5	16	50
It doesn't break.	5	16	50
Can turn it around.	5	14	49
You hide it.	5	15	50
Can put it over one eye.	5	14	49
It's shaped like a circle and it has two little round holes.	6	12	54
It's round on the front and flat on the back.	6	13	55
It's a fat button. [Q] Fat like a pancake.	9	1	58
A poker chip.	1	14	43
Take a string; tie it in a knot. [Q] It is sewed on.	5	21	51
Sew it on clothes. . . . If it comes loose, you fasten it back on.	5	13	49

be obvious to an experienced scorer. Some decisions may be purely pedantic, since if the responses were credited under different categories they would still receive the same credit. Other decisions, however, may affect the score by inflating or deflating the number of points allowed.

This table, Index to Some Scoring Decisions, lists some examples of Verbal Expression responses to each of the four test items. In the first column the number refers to the category under which the response is discussed in the following pages. In the second column the number refers to the example within the category. In the last column the page reference is listed.

In the following Discussion of Scoring Decisions the responses listed in Table 3 are discussed and the scoring is explained. The reader may wish to test himself on the unscored items in the table before reading the explanations of the author's considered scoring. In the Discussion of Scoring Decisions the following conventions have been used in the notations:

1. A *Q* in brackets indicates that the child's response was questioned by repeating the crucial part of the response, followed by "Tell me what you mean" or "Tell me more about that."

2. Ellipsis points between parts of the child's expression indicate that other remarks intervened between the two parts of the response.

3. Figures above certain words in the response indicate the category under which the child received credit. If the figure is in parentheses, the credit was given for adequate clarification following the examiner's question.

DISCUSSION OF SCORING DECISIONS

1. Label

1-1 (Block)
$$\overset{0}{} \quad \overset{0}{} \quad \overset{1}{}$$
"Shaped like a block"

> One must not be confused by the use of "shaped" and "like" here. This expression receives a credit for Label, not Comparison (9) or Shape (3). The block could be like a box or like an ice cube, but it *is* a block. (See Item 3-1.)

1-2 (Ball)
$$\overset{0}{} \quad \quad \quad \quad \overset{1}{}$$
"It's big." [Q] "Real big like a ball."

> "Ball" is given credit because, for this category only (Label), credit is allowed even following Q. (This rule is followed in order not to penalize the

more sophisticated child, who, it has been found, avoids the obvious statement of "This is a ball." See *Examiner's Manual* page 57.)

"Big" does not receive credit for the size of the ball unless, upon questioning as prescribed, the child says that it is larger than some other object. (See *Examiner's Manual* pages 53 and 57–58 and the scoring standards.)

1-3 (Block) "At bedtime you hide the block somewhere in your
$$
\begin{array}{cc} 0 & 1 \end{array}
$$
10
toys." (See Items 5-6, 10-5.)

1-4 (Ball)
$$
\begin{array}{cc} 5 & 10 \end{array}
$$
"Play ball." (See Item 10-1.)

1-5 (Ball)
$$
\begin{array}{cc} 5 & 0 \end{array}
$$
"Play baseball." (See Item 10-2.)

1-6 (Envelope)
$$
\begin{array}{ccc} 1 & 1 & 5 \end{array}
$$
"It's an envelope. . . . You use this stationery to write on."

It sometimes happens that a child will use both a label and a term indicating the class to which the object belongs. This is the only situation in which more than one point is allowed for this category. Thus, in the response given here, credit under Label is allowed for both "envelope" and "stationery." (See *Examiner's Manual* page 51.)

1-7 (Ball)
$$0$$
a. "It's a baseball."

$$1$$
b. "It's a ball thing."

Credit is denied in the first instance above because by being too specific the child has lost factuality, whereas "ball thing," by being so general, has maintained the basic concept.

1-8 (Envelope)
$$0$$
"It's a letter."

As indicated in the scoring standards, "a letter" does not receive credit under Label. The blank envelope obviously is not a letter although it could contain a letter. Neither does this response receive credit under Person, Place, or Thing (10) because the child is using the term to label the object. (See Item 10-9.)

	1	10	5

1-9 (Envelope)   "It's mail. . . . It comes in the mail. . . . You can mail it."

Note the differences in usage between these three expressions. When used to classify the envelope, the term "mail" is credited under Label; when used in relation to the delivery of mail it is credited under Person, Place, or Thing (10); when used as a verb it is credited under Function (5). The same protocol may receive all three credits. (See *Examiner's Manual* page 56.)

	0	0 1

1-10 (Ball)   "My brother has a great big ball."

Although this remark refers to an irrelevant object (not the object at hand) the label "ball" is given credit in order not to penalize the more sophisticated child who would not label the object. (See *Examiner's Manual* page 55.)

	1	7 6

1-11 (Button)   a. "Some buttons have four holes."

	1	0 0

b. "My buttons have four holes."

Although credit is not given for reference to extraneous objects (since they are not relevant to the object at hand), credit is allowed for responses which generalize to the group of objects as a whole. Thus, in the first statement above the child has implied that this button belongs to a larger class of buttons, some of which have four holes. In the second statement the child has been sidetracked, referring to a specific button other than the one at hand.

A perusal of the scoring standards gives examples of this, such as:

2
"Sometimes they're brown." (envelopes, *Examiner's Manual* page 66.)

1   6
"Some buttons don't have holes." (*Examiner's Manual* page 68.)

2
"They can be lots of colors." (blocks, *Examiner's Manual* page 64.)

In the sole category of Label credit is allowed even in statements not referring to the object at hand. This credit is to compensate for the fact that sophisticated subjects hesitate to make such an obvious statement as "This is a button."

                        5

1-12 (Button)   "It is for to button." (See Item 5-20.)

                 0   5   10

1-13 (Envelope) "It's a paper for putting letters in." (See Item 4-4.)

                 0

1-14 (Button)   "A poker chip."

This should be questioned in case the child means "like a poker chip." As it stands, of course, it cannot receive any credit.

2. Color

                 2   1

2-1 (Ball)   "It's a blue ball."

Use of any color name, whether factual or not, is credited. (See *Examiner's Manual* pages 51–52.) Since children below five years of age frequently do not know color names, the child is given credit for communicating the concept of color and recognizing that colors do have names.

                 2

2-2 (Block)   "What color is it?"

The child is given credit (as above) for communicating the concept of color. Interrogative and negative responses are scored in the same manner as are declarative responses. (During administration the examiner throws the question back to the child by saying "What do *you* think?" in response to this question.)

                 2   8

2-3 (Button)   "It's white. . . . It's clear."

The child receives two points here, since the term "clear" signifies transparency, not color. (See scoring standards.)

                 2   0

2-4 (Ball)   "It's green. . . . It's red."

Only one point is allowed for reference to color. (See *Examiner's Manual* page 52.)

2-5 (Envelope) $\overset{2}{\text{"It's yellow}} \ldots \overset{2}{\text{white."}}$ [Q] "The glue is yellow and
the paper is white."

An additional point is allowed for the color of
an acceptable major part. If there is any doubt, the
examiner should question.

---

3. Shape

3-1 (Ball) $\overset{0}{\text{a.}} \overset{0}{\text{"Shaped}} \overset{1}{\text{like a ball."}}$

$\overset{0}{\text{b.}} \overset{0}{\text{"Shaped}} \overset{3}{\text{like a circle."}}$

If the child uses an acceptable name for the item
(see scoring standards) he receives credit under
Label (1). If he uses an acceptable geometric term
he receives credit under Shape. He does not receive
credit for the mere use of the term "shape."

One must not be confused here by the use of the
term "like." Such an expression receives a credit for
either Label (1) or Shape, but not for Comparison
(9). (See *Examiner's Manual* pages 52 and 53–54.)

3-2 (Block) $\overset{3}{\text{"A square head"}} \overset{0}{\text{[Q]}}$ "Can hammer it square." (See
Item 9-5.)

3-3 (Button) $\overset{(3)}{\text{a.}} \overset{1}{\text{"It's a fat button."}}$ [Q] "It's round."

$\overset{(8)}{\text{b.}} \overset{1}{\text{"It's a fat button."}}$ [Q] "It's big."

$\overset{0}{\text{c.}} \overset{1}{\text{"It's a fat button."}}$ [Q] "It's real fat."

$\overset{0}{\text{(Block)}}$ d. "It's fat." (See Item 8-1.)

3-4 (Block) $\overset{6}{\text{"The corners}} \overset{0}{\text{are round."}}$

Basically, the corners of the block are sharp or
pointed, not round. If some corners are somewhat
rounded, this should be considered an accidental
detail and reference to it denied credit.

3-5 (Ball) $\overset{3}{\text{"There is a}} \overset{0}{\text{round thing}} \overset{1}{\text{around the ball."}}$ [Q] (repeated same)

The child was probably referring to the midline of
the ball, but his verbal expression was not adequate

enough to provide a more definite term than "thing." "Round" receives credit under Shape. It is very easy to make the mistake of denying credit for the term which modifies a word not receiving credit. It is like the grin on the face of the Cheshire cat in *Alice in Wonderland*. You must credit the grin, even though you can't see the face.

3-6 (Button)

$$\overset{7}{} \quad \overset{6}{} \qquad \overset{0}{} \qquad \overset{0}{}$$
"It's got two holes in the center and another hole
$$\overset{9}{} \qquad \overset{0}{}$$
almost like a triangle, something like a boat." (See Item 6-11.)

4. Composition

4-1 (Ball)

$$\overset{4}{} \qquad\qquad\qquad \overset{0}{}$$
"It's rubber. . . . It's something like plastic."

This expression is tantamount to saying that the ball is made out of "something like plastic" and is redundant to "rubber," which has already been credited. Only one point is allowed for reference to composition.

4-2 (Block)

$$\overset{0}{}$$
"Made out of brick."

Much leniency is allowed for the category of Composition, but this is too far from factual. Even "rubber" and "plastic" are not given credit in the scoring standards for the block.

4-3 (Envelope)

$$\overset{4}{} \qquad\qquad\qquad \overset{0}{}$$
"It's paper . . . made out of wood."

Either, but not both, of these statements receives credit. Only one point is allowed for reference to composition except that an additional point may be allowed for the composition of a major part; for example, "glue" in addition to "paper."

4-4 (Envelope)

$$\overset{0}{} \qquad \overset{5}{} \quad \overset{10}{}$$
"It's a paper for putting letters in."

"Paper" is too generalized a term to receive credit for Label (1) and is not used by the child to indicate composition, so credit is denied. Of course, "putting letters in" receives credit for Function (5) and for Person, Place, or Thing (10).

(6)   0   1

4-5 (Button)   "It's got a funny thing." [Q] "The glass button's got
a bump around it." (See Item 6-7.)

8   0

4-6 (Block)   a. "It's made out of hard stuff." [Q] "It's real hard."

8   (4)

b. "It's made out of hard stuff." [Q] "Hard stuff like
wood."

Note the difference in scoring these alternative
statements. In the first statement no qualifying remarks were added after questioning; therefore, no
credit is given for "stuff." In the second statement
composition was specified, so credit was allowed for
"stuff."

(4)

4-7 (Ball)   "Claydough." [Q] "Made out of claydough."

This is given credit for Composition since the term
would seem to be a confusion of "clay" and "Play-
dough," either of which is within the realm of approximate factuality. The question was necessary
to make sure the child was not labelling the ball as
"claydough," in which case he would have received
no credit. He might also have said it was "like claydough," creditable under Comparison (9).

5. Function

10   5

5-1 (Ball)   "The dog chews it."

"Chews" is not listed under Category 5 in the
scoring standards and in relation to babies and children would not be considered a specific function of
the ball. The action involved where a dog is con-
cerned, however, is specifically that of chasing or
chewing; and since "dog" is accepted under Category 10, the function "chews" must receive credit
under Category 5.

0

5-2 (Ball)   "They bust." [Q] "Get a nail and stick it in it and
it gets flat."

Some leniency is allowed for factuality, but since
in the scoring standards credit is given under Other
Physical Characteristics (8) for "solid, not hollow,

not empty," it was not considered logical to give credit for "they bust" or "it gets flat," as if the ball were a balloon. Because of the spongy nature of the ball, credit may still be given for "air in it" (Composition, Category 4), as indicated in the scoring standards.

5-3 (Block)   a. "It doesn't bounce."
                                     5

(Ball)   b. "Can't hear nothing in it."
                                     5

These negative responses warrant credit as statements of fact describing what the item is not like or does not do. (See *Examiner's Manual* page 58.) The block does not bounce as did the ball the child has just been asked to tell about. If he perseveres later and gives the same response to all items, as sometimes happens, it seems reasonable to deny the later credits but allow the one for block. "Can't hear nothing in it" describes what the ball is not like — some babies' balls do rattle.

5-4 (Ball)   "It's a bouncing ball."
                          5   1

"Bouncing," as a form of the verb "to bounce," is given credit as a function or action of the. ball rather than a physical characteristic. Other responses in the scoring standards have comparable credit under Category 5 for such responses as "playing blocks" and "mailing envelope."
                                               5
                    1   5   1

5-5 (Block)   "Can turn it over and it will stay in place."
                      0   0

This is not specific enough to receive credit as it stands but should be questioned. Most things can be turned over and will stay in place. The child probably means that the block won't roll like the ball, and if he says that, following questioning, he should receive credit for "stay in place."

5-6 (Block)   "Hide it in the playroom."
                      0   10

"Hide" is not a specific function of a block any more than of many other things. It applies universally to any small object. "Playroom," of course, is closely associated with blocks and other toys and is so specified under Category 10 in the scoring standards.

5-7 (Envelope)

        10   5

"It's to not let the letter fall out." [Q] "Lick it right here and it sticks."

The specific function of the flap of an envelope is "to not let the letter fall out." It therefore receives credit under Category 5. "Letter," of course, is closely associated with the envelope and receives credit under Category 10. Questioning may have denied the child further credit.

5-8 (Envelope)

    0   10

"To put a valentine there." [Q] (no response)

The term "put" is such a generalized, nonspecific word that it does not receive credit in most situations. "Put the ball in the box," "Put the block away," "Put the button on a string," and "Put the envelope here" are too vague to receive credit. "Put a letter in" is given credit for the envelope only because the term "Put in" is synonymous with "insert," which, after all, is the main function of an envelope.

5-9 (Envelope)

    (9)

a. "Can make a house." [Q] "With this up."

    (9)

b. "Can make a plane." [Q] "You fold it."

    (9)

c. "Can make paper dolls." [Q] "Cut them out with scissors." (See Item 9-12.)

5-10 (Envelope)

    5

"Can squash it."

This is credited since it is equivalent to "Can crumple it" or "Can wrinkle it."

5-11 (Envelope)

    5   10   5   10

"Can put a letter in it. . . . It holds money."

As indicated in the scoring standards, both "put in" and "holds" are given credit under Function, since so many children discriminate between these different functions of an envelope. Envelopes are used (a) to put letters in, (b) to store such things as rubber bands, paper clips, coins, and so on, and also (c) to carry things back and forth to school (milk money, etc.).

5-12 (Envelope) "You read it."
5

No such function is mentioned in the scoring standards, but credit here seems just as valid as for the other functions listed. After all, why write on an envelope if no one reads it?

5-13 (Button)
5   10   5   0
a. "Sew it on clothes. . . . If it comes loose, you fastens it back on."

5   10   5
b. "Holds clothes together. . . . If it comes loose, you
5
fasten it back on."

5   10   5
c. "Fastens clothes together. . . . If it comes loose,
5
you sew it back on."

5   10   5
d. "Fastens clothes together. . . . If it comes loose,
0
you fasten it back on."

In scoring these three responses, redundancy of vocabulary as well as redundancy of ideas must be considered. "Fastens" and "sews" are listed as redundant to each other in the scoring standards when they refer to the same function as in *a* above. However, in the other three responses there are two separate functions mentioned — one is holding clothes together, and the other is attaching the button. If different words are used for these two functions, as in *b* and *c* above, they each receive credit. If the same word is used (even though referring to different functions) only one may be credited, as in *d*. Use of the same term never receives more than one point credit *in any one category* for a given object.

5-14 (Button)
0
a. "Can turn it around."

0   0
b. "Can put it over one eye."

These responses should be questioned. They are too indefinite to receive credit as they stand, but the

child may have had creditable concepts in mind.
"Can turn it around" may have contained the concept of spinning, which is noted under Function in
the scoring standards. "Can put it over one eye"
may have implied playing with it as a monacle
(Comparison, Category 9) or using it as a peephole
(Function, Category 5). (See Item 7-2 for denial
of credit for "one.")

5-15 (Button)   5
                "You hide it."

Although this response does not receive credit for
the other objects (too universal), it does receive
credit for the button, since at least one game specifically uses the button for hiding (Button, Button,
Who Has the Button?). This is so specified in the
scoring standards.

5-16 (Button)   5
                a. "You can break it."

                5
                b. "It doesn't break.

Plastic buttons do not break easily, but glass buttons do. Since both "glass" and "plastic" are acceptable terms for Composition (4), either "It breaks" or
"It doesn't break" may be credited (but, of course,
only one of them).

5-17 (Envelope)   0   10   0
                "Write a letter to your Grandma."

Credit is given for "write" only if it refers to the
envelope, not when used with reference to the letter
put into the envelope. This is specified under "0
Points" in the scoring standards.

"Letter," of course, receives credit under Person,
Place, or Thing (10) regardless of the creditability of
"write." "Grandma" is too specific (friend, Grandma,
Santa Claus) to receive credit.

5-18 (Ball)   0
                "You can bowl with it."

Some limits had to be set about how similar another ball has to be to the little jack ball in order to
receive credit. A bowling ball is obviously too far
removed and, therefore, no credit is given for the
function "bowl."

5-19 (Ball)
          5   10
"Can play ping-pong with it."

Considering the size and weight of the ball, this response falls within the realm of the possible and is given credit for Function and for Person, Place, or Thing (10) as completing the action of "play."

5-20 (Button)
          5
"It's for to button."

Although grammatically inadequate, this response leaves no doubt as to its meaning and receives credit for Function, not Label (1).

5-21 (Button)
          10
"Take a string; tie it in a knot." [Q] "It is sewed on."

No credit is given for Function here, since no term preceding the question indicated a function of the button.

6. Major Parts

6-1 (Ball)
          3   0   1
"There is a round thing around the ball." [Q] (repeated same) (See Item 3-5.)

6-2 (Block)
          7   3   0
"Has ten flat places." [Q] "Ten flat parts."
          7   3 (6)
"Has ten flat places." [Q] "Ten squares."
          7   3   0   0
"Has ten flat places." [Q] "Ten square parts."

"Ten" and "flat" receive credit for Numerosity (7) and Shape (3), respectively, but unless the child gives a definitive name for the major part after questioning, the indefinite term does not receive credit. If, after questioning, he responds "ten squares," he receives credit for the term "places," since in the scoring standards "squares" is listed under Major Parts. If he says "ten square parts," no credit is given for either "square" (a new concept following Q) or for "parts" (not a creditable name for that major part as specified on *Examiner's Manual* pages 52–53).

6-3 (Button)
          8   0   5
"It has a little place to sew through." [Q] "Here, see?"

The term "place" is not definitive enough to receive credit for Major Parts, but since the hole is described by function ("to sew through") the child is given credit under Category 5. (See *Examiner's Manual* pages 52–53.)

It is easy to overlook a creditable term which characterizes a noncreditable term. Although "place" for the hole is too indefinite to receive credit, the acceptable characteristic of "little" should receive credit under Category 8.

Although there are possibly some instances when a second question may be appropriate, it should be allowed sparingly. In this case it would not be appropriate to question "here." The child has already indicated his paucity of verbal expression, and credit for words dragged out of him would be misleading.

3   0

6-4 (Block)   "Flat on all ends."

It is possible that the child meant "sides" when he said "ends." However, "ends" is specified in the scoring standards as receiving no credit since it is not appropriate to a square object.

8   0

6-5 (Block)   "It's real sharp here." [Q] (pointed)

No credit is allowed for "here" although the child pointed to the corner. Gestures are ignored in scoring the Verbal Expression test; the examiner should be able to score the responses if he were blind.

The child is given credit under Other Physical Characteristics (8) for "sharp," even though the corner was not labelled as such.

9   (6)

6-6 (Envelope)   "It looks like a house with this up." [Q] "Hold the flap up and it looks like a house."

The examiner questioned the term "this." (E: "With *this* up? Tell me what you mean.") Since the child then used a creditable term for the major part ("flap"), he is given credit for "this."

The comparison to a house was given credit because of similarity of shape.

6-7 (Button)

(6)   0   1
"It's got a funny thing." [Q] "The glass button's got a bump around it."

The term "thing" was questioned and receives credit as a major part because it is adequately explained by "bump around it."

No credit was allowed for the Composition (4) because "glass" was introduced only after the Q. The category of Label (1), however, is different in that credit is allowed after Q. (See Scoring Instructions, *Examiner's Manual* page 57.)

6-8 (Envelope)

7 6   0   9
"It's got four corners and a thing like a tent." [Q] "A piece that folds over."

"Thing" does not receive credit for the flap because even after questioning, the child did not give a creditable name for the "piece that folds over." He described the "thing" by its function, but since this description follows Q, it receives no credit for Function. If the term "folds over" had occurred before the Q, it would have received credit for Function (5) but not for Major Parts. (See *Examiner's Manual* pages 52–53: Major Parts.)

The comparison "like a tent" stands by itself, and the credit for Comparison (9) is not contingent upon credit for "thing." The credits for Numerosity (7) and Major Parts speak for themselves.

6-9 (Button)

8 0   9
"It's got a little thing like a little football." [Q] "This."

This child did not name the elliptical hollow except by comparison to a football. Therefore, he receives no credit for Major Parts, but a credit for Comparison (9). He also receives a credit under Other Physical Characteristics (8) for noting the size of the part he did not name definitely.

6-10 (Envelope)

6
"It has a hole." [Q] "An open place here."

The term "hole" must be accepted for the opening or slit as the major part since a "hole" is defined as "an opening into something." The response was

questioned to make sure that the child was not referring to some accidental detail.

6-11 (Button)

       7   6   0   0
"It's got two holes in the center and another hole
             9   0
almost like a triangle, something like a boat."

There are several points to be considered in this
response. "Two holes," of course, receives two points,
one each for Numerosity (7) and Major Parts.
"Center" is too universal to receive credit, as indicated in the scoring standards. The second use of
"hole," although referring to a second major part,
cannot receive credit because that term has already
been given credit in the same category. A synonym
such as "hollow" or "groove" would have received
credit for the second "hole," but no credit is given
the *same term* in the *same category*. (See *Examiner's
Manual* page 56.) Redundancy of vocabulary as well
as redundancy of concept must be considered.

In referring to the elliptical hollow on the button,
the child appears to have been groping for a descrip-
tive term — "almost like a triangle, something like
a boat." Since both of these comparisons were based
on the same concept (shape), only one point of
credit is given.

6-12 (Button)

        3   7 8   0   6
a. "It's round and it has two little round holes."
                         3   7   8
b. "It's shaped like a circle and it has two little
    3   6
round holes."

If the same term is used twice, as in *a* above, it
receives only one point *in the same category* even
though it refers to different parts. If credited *in different categories,* however, identical terms may be
credited twice, as in Item 1-9. (Note the distinction
made between "Repetitive responses" and "Other
redundant responses" on *Examiner's Manual* page
56.)

The terms "round" and "circle" are redundant to
each other when modifying the same object or the
same major part. In contrast, such synonyms may

receive separate points, as in *b* above, when referring to different parts of the object and/or the object itself. (See discussion under Item 5-13.)

6-13 (Button)

         3   0   3   0

a. "It's round on the top and flat on the bottom."

         3   6   3   6

b. "It's round on the front and flat on the back."

As specified in the scoring standards, "top" and "bottom" do not receive credit because these terms do not relate to the button itself but only to its position. When the button is turned over, the top becomes the bottom and the bottom becomes the top. The "front" and "back" of the button are genuine parts of the button and have been specified as major parts.

7. Numerosity

7-1 (Block)

         8   0   6

a. "It is sharp on one corner."

         7   8

b. "It is one inch high."

         0   2

c. "This one is green."

In *a* the term "one" is not credited for Numerosity since it does not fall within the limits of one-half to twice the actual number of corners. In *c* the term "one" does not receive credit because it is used as a pronoun referring to the object rather than as an indicator of numerosity. (See Item 8-5.)

7-2 (Button)

         5   0

"You can look through it with one eye."

The term "one" in this instance does not refer to the object at hand (the button); it does not fit the arbitrary definition of relevant.

7-3 (Envelope)

         7   7

"It's four inches by six inches."

         7   7

"It's four by six."

(Block)

         7

"It's about one inch."

         7   0   0

"It's one by one by one."

Credit is allowed for numerals referring to the size

of any dimension, and additional credit is allowed for reference to a different dimension, but only if the numeral used is different from the first. (See Item 8-5.)

$$7 \quad 8 \quad 6 \qquad 0 \qquad 0$$

7-4 (Block)   "It has six sharp corners but these two are round."

The term "two" receives no credit for Numerosity since only one point is given for reference to any one dimension or major part. (See Item 3-4 for denial of credit to "round.")

8. Other Physical Characteristics

	(3) 1
8-1 (Button)	a. "It's a fat button." [Q] "It's round."
	(8) 1
	b. "It's a fat button." [Q] "It's big."
	0 1
	c. "It's a fat button." [Q] "It's real fat."
	0
(Block)	d. "It's fat."

The word "fat" is used ambiguously by children. They sometimes erroneously use it to refer to size, meaning "big" (Other Physical Characteristics), or to shape, meaning "round" rather than "plump." Most properly it is used to mean plump or well filled out. Thus, it is given credit under Shape (3) when referring to the ball (redundant to "round" or "spherical"). But the button is not "fat," and only if the child clarifies the term as meaning "round" is it given credit under Shape (3). If he clarifies it as meaning "big" it is given credit under Other Physical Characteristics. If it is not clarified at all, it receives no credit.

"Fat" does not receive credit for the shape of a block. The block is neither round nor big nor plump.

$$5 \qquad 1$$

8-2 (Ball)   "It's a bouncing ball." (See Item 5-4.)

$$6 \qquad 8$$

8-3 (Block)   "Each side is the same size."

"The same size" is credited under Other Physical Characteristics because it characterizes the uniformity of "sides," which receives credit under Major Parts (6).

(8)
8-4 (Block)   "It's soft." [Q] "Smooth when you rub it."

The term "soft" has two distinctive meanings; it is the opposite of both "hard" and "rough." It is therefore necessary to question the child when he uses the term "soft" lest he also use one of its opposites. Since "hard" and "soft" are opposites, the child cannot be given credit for both unless he indicates that he is talking about the smoothness of the object when he uses the term "soft." (See *Examiner's Manual* page 58.)

	7 8

8-5 (Ball)   a. "It's one inch across."

     7   8
(Block)   b. "It's one inch high."

     7   8   0   8
c. "It's about one inch high and one inch wide."

     7   8   7   8
(Envelope)   d. "It's two inches wide and four inches long."

     7   8   0
e. "It's about six inches long; it could be ten inches
     0
long."

Delineation of dimension receives credit under Other Physical Characteristics. If more than one dimension is mentioned, each receives credit. This is in addition to any credit for Numerosity (7) which is allowed for discrete numerals that are within the allowable limits of one-half to twice the actual measurement. (See Item 7-3.)

     8   0
8-6 (Envelope)   "It's real sharp here." [Q] (pointed)

The term "here" is an ambiguous response and was questioned to clarify the location as if the examiner were blind. The physical characteristic of sharpness is not contingent upon a creditable term for the corner, and the response is therefore given credit for Other Physical Characteristics.

     0
8-7 (Envelope)   "It's wrinkled."

No matter how factual this may be, it does not receive credit. It is irrelevant because it does not apply to the envelopes in other kits. It merely indicates that the examiner should replace the envelope in his kit.

8-8 (Button)   "It's white. . . . It's clear." (See Item 2-3.)

The numbers above the quote: 2 (over "white") 8 (over "clear")

9. Comparison

9-1 (Button)   "It's a fat button." [Q] "Fat like a pancake."

Numbers above: 0 (over "fat") 1 (over "like")

No credit is given for Comparison since "like a pancake" follows Q. No credit is given for "fat" since comparing it to a pancake does not clarify what the child mean by "fat."

The examiner should explore the possibility of a speech defect and whether or not the child was saying "flat like a pancake," in which case he would have recieved credit for Shape (3). (See Item 3-3.)

9-2 (Button)   "It's got a little thing like a little football." [Q] "This." (See Item 6-9.)

Numbers above: 8 (over "got") 0 (over "thing") 0 (over "like") 9 (over "football")

9-3 (Envelope)   "It's got four corners and a thing like a tent." [Q] "A piece that folds over." (See Item 6-8.)

Numbers above: 7 (over "got") 6 (over "corners") 0 (over "thing") 9 (over "tent")

9-4 (Block)   "For a light on the top of a fire engine."

Numbers above: 0 (over "light") 0 (over "fire engine")

This response should have been questioned to see if the child could specify some characteristic of the block which would justify crediting the comparison. The examiner must not project his own creativity or deny a concept which might be creditable upon clarification. *Give credit to the child's creativity only if it can be adequately expressed.*

9-5 (Block)   "A square head." [Q] "You can hammer it square."

Numbers above: 3 (over "square") 0 (over "head")

"Square" is accepted for the shape even though no credit can be given for "head" either as Label (1) or as Comparison. Perhaps a head could be hammered until it is square, but that is far-fetched and irrelevant.

9-6 (Ball)   "It's a round head." [Q] "Like a puppet."

Numbers above: 3 (over "round") (9) (over "head")

If this had not been questioned it could hardly receive credit for "head" under Comparison since the child did not clearly indicate the relationship until after Q. Credit was given for "round" both as the shape of the ball and the basis for the comparison.

9-7 (Ball)　　　　"You can bowl with it." (See Item 5-18.)

9-8 (Block)　　　　"Shaped like a block." (See Items 1-1 and 3-1.)

9-9 (Button)　　　　"It's got two holes in the center and another hole almost like a triangle, something like a boat." (See Item 6-11.)

9-10 (Ball)　　　　"It's rubber. . . . It's something like plastic." (See Item 4-1.)

9-11 (Button)　　　　"A poker chip." (See Item 1-14.)

9-12 (Envelope)　　　"Can make a house." [Q] "With this up."

"Can make a plane." [Q] "You fold it."

"Can make paper dolls." [Q] "Cut them out with scissors."

As stated on *Examiner's Manual* pages 53–54, the category of Comparison includes "responses which state what the object could be if certain specified changes were made." Many children respond to the envelope by stating, "You can make an airplane," or "You can make a house." Such responses are given credit under Comparison. The examiner often has to question to make sure he understands the basis of the comparison or the nature of the changes.

10. Person, Place, or Thing

10-1 (Ball)　　　　"Play ball."

The word "ball" as used here is not a label as in "Play with the ball," or "This is a ball." Instead, it completes the action of the verb "play" and is credited under the category of Person, Place, or Thing. It is redundant to "Play jacks" and "Play catch."

10-2 (Ball)

$\overset{5}{}\quad\overset{0}{}$

"Play baseball."

As indicated in the scoring standards, the term "baseball," whether used as a label or complement of "play," receives no credit. By being so specific in the erroneous kind of game played, the child has shown a lack of factuality. If the child draws a comparison to a baseball, of course, he receives credit under Category 9.

10-3 (Ball)

$\overset{0}{}\qquad\qquad\overset{0}{}\quad\overset{5}{}$

"People and animals play with it."

In the scoring standards "people" is specified as an uncreditable response and therefore receives no credit. Likewise, "animals" receives no credit because it is too inclusive a term. Cats and dogs play with a ball, but the majority of animals do not. The verb "play" expresses a creditable concept and receives credit without knowledge of who plays.

10-4 (Ball)

$\overset{5}{}\qquad\qquad\overset{0}{}\quad\overset{10}{}\qquad\overset{0}{}$

"When you throw it on the roof, the dog can't get it."

"Thow" is a function (Category 5) of the ball, but "the roof" is not specifically associated with the ball any more than the sidewalk, the grass, or the table is. Credit is specified for "dog," but "get" is too general a word — too universal.

10-5 (Block)

$\overset{0}{}\qquad\qquad\qquad\overset{10}{}$

"At bedtime you can hide it somewhere in your toys."

"Toys" receives credit under Person, Place, or Thing because a block is certainly closely associated with other toys. Since the term "toys" would have received a credit for classification if used as a label, it is important to consider the sense in which a term is used. In this case it does not refer to the block but to other toys.

"Hide it" does not receive credit because it applies too universally. You can hide any reasonably sized object. (See Item 5-6.)

10-6 (Envelope)

$\overset{9}{}$

"Can make a house." [Q] "With this up."

$\overset{9}{}$

"Can make a plane." [Q] "You fold it."

9
"Can make paper dolls." [Q] "Cut them out with
scissors." (See Item 9-12.)

10-7 (Button)

0 10 0 5   10
"Put it on your shirt or use it to button up your coat."
"Shirt" and "coat" are listed in the scoring standards as being redundant to each other and in common situations would receive only one point. In dis-
cussing "Other redundant responses," however, the
Examiner's Manual (page 56) specifically states:
"Such redundant terms may each receive additional
credit in a single category only if (a) they refer to
discrete characteristics (such as major parts) of the
object, or (b) they complete discrete action terms."
Thus, "shirt" receives credit for completing the
action verb "put on," and "coat" also receives credit
because it completes a different action term, "button
up."

10-8 (Envelope)

1   10   5
"It's mail. . . . It comes in the mail. . . . You can mail
it." (See Item 1-9.)

10-9 (Envelope)

0
"It's a letter." (See Item 1-8.)

V

Precautions in Administering the Grammatic Closure Subtest

The Grammatic Closure subtest is presented very simply, since the expressions used by the examiner are printed on the test booklet for him to read. He points to the appropriate pictures as he reads the given statements, emphasizing the underscored words and stopping abruptly at the point where the child is to supply the missing words. It is a test to assess the child's ability to predict the proper grammatic form. It measures the form rather than the content of the missing word since the content has been kept simple and is provided for the child both verbally and graphically.

WHEN TO REPEAT ITEMS

In evaluating the child's response, the examiner must keep in mind that he is trying to find out if the child can predict a particular form of a particular word as used in everyday language. Therefore, if in his response the child does not use *some* form of that particular word, he is given a second chance. If he uses *any* form of that word, no second chance is given. The anticipated words in another form are presented in the sentence read by the examiner, and correct responses are indicated in the first column of the scoring standards. Some clearly incorrect responses are indicated in the last column of the scoring standards, and some common noncommittal responses are presented in the middle column (repeat items).

For those examiners who have difficulty in knowing when to repeat the item, Figure 1 may give them a graphic reminder. Repetition is dependent not upon the correctness or incorrectness of the response but only upon whether or not the child used *any* form of the key word in the stimulus sentence read by the examiner.

DUAL USE OF SOME PICTURES

There is another spot in this subtest which causes some examiners difficulty. This is the situation in which two consecutive test items are

Figure 1. When to Repeat Items on the Grammatic Closure Subtest

Ask yourself: Did the child use *any* form of the anticipated word?

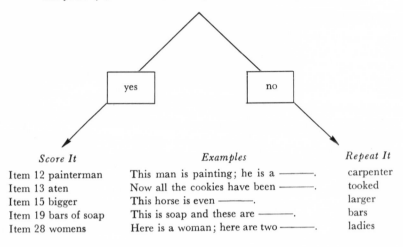

Score It	Examples	Repeat It
Item 12 painterman	This man is painting; he is a ————.	carpenter
Item 13 aten	Now all the cookies have been ————.	tooked
Item 15 bigger	This horse is even ————.	larger
Item 19 bars of soap	This is soap and these are ————.	bars
Item 28 womens	Here is a woman; here are two ————.	ladies

presented with the same picture. In some of these situations there is no problem since the two items are independent of each other. There are three item pairs, however, that require an adaptation of the usual presentation. Look at the directions on *Examiner's Manual* page 71. In the following quotation, the bracketed expressions have been added to clarify the directions:

Members of Item pairs 15–16 [the horses], 20–21 [the blocks], and 24–25 [the cookies] are dependent on each other and repetition is therefore somewhat different. On the first item of any pair ["bigger" for Item 15, "more" for Item 20, and "better" for Item 24], when no form of the anticipated word is used [by the child], all material up to and including the incomplete statement is repeated [by E]. [For example, "This horse is *not big*. This horse *is big*. This horse is even ————.] On the second item in the pair [when repetition is necessary], material *excluding E's first incomplete statement* is repeated.

In such a manner the following exchange might occur:

Item 15 E: "This horse is *not big*. This horse *is big*. This horse is even _____."

S: "More big." [Incorrect form of anticipated word.]

Item 16 E: "And this horse is the very _____."

S: "He's got spots."

E: "No, this horse is *not big*. This horse *is big*. [Skip "This horse is even more big."] And this horse is the very _____."

S: "Most big."

When the child has failed Item 15 on both trials and has not given any form of the anticipated word on the first trial of Item 16, the above adaptation must be made in order to avoid giving the child a clue to the expected response on his second trial of Item 16. The examiner *must not correct* the child's mistake on Item 15, and he *must not repeat* the child's incorrect response. The correct alternative is to skip that item altogether.

VI

Precautions in Administering the Sound Blending Subtest

The purpose of this subtest is to discover those children who have a specific disability in sound blending. Most children learn incidentally the art of blending isolated sounds to form a word. The child who does not do this automatically and has not been taught to do so may become a casualty in the reading program. It is these children whom the Sound Blending subtest attempts to discover.

There are two aspects of this sound blending ability: one is analytic, and the other is synthetic. One requires the ability to break down a word into its component sounds; the other requires the ability to put sounds together. In administering the Sound Blending test, you must use the analytic aspect while the child uses the synthetic aspect. Some examiners have difficulty in breaking down the word into its component sounds so that the child can hear the same sounds that are in the word. (It is, of course, impossible to create the identical sounds in isolation that occur in the word. In actual words, for example, the initial /p/ in *pat* is not actually the same as the final /p/ in *map*. The /b/ sound in isolation is not identical to the /b/ sound in a word.) It is very important that the examiner "hear" the sounds in the word so that he can make each isolated sound as near as possible to the sound in the word.

Note the following precautions for the administration of this subtest:

1. If you have any doubt about your understanding of the test or about your ability to adequately present the words properly broken down, by all means seek the help of a competent speech correctionist or phonetician. Not all teachers who teach phonics in the elementary school do an adequate job of presenting the sounds.

2. Even if you think you have mastered the art of presenting this test, listen occasionally to the record of sound blending which is included in each test kit. You may want to sound along with the record to practice the sounds and the timing.

3. Remember to isolate the sounds that you hear, not the symbols

that you see. The sounds in *nose* are /n - ō - z/ rather than /n - ō - s - e/. The word *feather* does not have a /th/ sound like that in *think,* but a /th/ sound like the one in *those.*

4. Be careful to avoid the audible grunt that is difficult to avoid at the end of such sounds as /b/ and /g/ and /d/ presented in isolation. The vibration of the larynx must not be allowed to continue after the lips or throat are opened. If the vibration of the larynx occurs before and just as the throat or lips are opened, the distinctive sound will be audible. In contrast to this, the /r/ sound must be somewhat prolonged and started and stopped as gently as possible to avoid either /er/ or /ruh/.

5. The examiner should note certain conventions in the administration of this test that are sometimes overlooked:

a. In Section A of the test it is imperative that the child *verbalize,* not merely point to, the appropriate picture. This should be insisted upon in the demonstration and also on the test items.

b. When Section A is used all seven items must be administered. If the child is successful on *any one item,* Section B is administered.

c. When beginning with Section B of the test (for children 6-0 and above), the examiner should drop back to Section A if and when the child fails one of the first three items of Section B (Item 8, or 9, or 10).

d. The examiner should carefully note the following ceiling requirements:

Section A: If *no* items are passed, the test is discontinued (unless a child over six has passed any of Items 8, 9, or 10).

Section B: If three consecutive errors are made *prior to or including* Item 18, the test is discontinued.

Section C: If three consecutive errors are made *after* Item 18, only Section B is discontinued, but Section C must be administered until three consecutive errors are made in that section.

e. *No repetition* of the test items is allowed. As noted on *Examiner's Manual* page 18, "Repetition of items is permissible with the exception of (a) the two sequential memory tests and the Sound Blending Test, where no repetition is allowed, and (b) the Auditory Closure Test, where only a single repetition is allowed."

f. On demonstration items, the examiner should be careful not to train sound blending ability — only to make sure the child understands the task. As noted on *Examiner's Manual* page 18, "On the Sound Blending Test only the prescribed demonstration should be given since this skill may be susceptible to training."

VII

Questions and Answers

Since the ITPA was revised in 1968, many questions have been asked by those who have used the test. Although many of the questions received could have been answered by a careful reading of the *Examiner's Manual* (1968) and Paraskevopoulos and Kirk (1969), an effort is made here to answer some of the most common questions. Another book, entitled *Psycholinguistic Learning Disabilities: Diagnosis and Remediation* (Kirk and Kirk), was published in 1971 to further clarify the scope and purpose of the ITPA. Additional publications are now being prepared which will review the research results of current studies.

This chapter has been prepared to answer briefly (a) some questions related to general administration and scoring of the ITPA, (b) specific questions related to some of the subtests, and (c) questions related to the general use and interpretation of the ITPA.

GENERAL QUESTIONS ABOUT ADMINISTRATION AND SCORING

Q: *Must the ITPA be administered in one sitting?*

A: No. With young children or easily distracted children it is often necessary to give the test in two sittings. No more than one week should elapse between the first and second sittings. Especially when a new examiner is slow in completing the test is it necessary to break the test into two sessions.

Q: *Must the subtests be given in the order presented in the* Examiner's Manual?

A: This was the order used in the standardization; therefore, it is best to follow the prescribed order. The tests were arranged in this order to avoid mental set, to provide maximum interest, and to prevent fatigue. Tests of the same process, for example, were separated, and the Visual Sequential Memory test was placed early in the program since it demands more prolonged attention.

Q: *Must a tester give all twelve subtests if he feels it is not necessary for a particular child?*

A: We recommend that the ten basic subtests be given each child in order to have a reference point (composite score or mean scaled score) against which to compare each subtest score. The interpretation for a child who is low on some and high on others is quite different from that for one who is low straight across the board. Much of the interpretation depends upon the *pattern* of the scores a child achieves, and the deviations among the child's own abilities are more important than any deviation from the norms representing average children. The two supplementary subtests are not included in the composite score and are of particular value (a) in clinical evaluation of reading problems and (b) as a supplementary evaluation of the automatic ability to integrate auditory stimuli.

In diagnosing learning disabilities one must determine whether the child has a general disability or a specific disability. You may wish to have scores in other areas with which to compare the child's scores in the areas of deficiency. For this purpose you must take into account the reliability of the differences between subtest scores rather than accepting each score as an exact point regardless of errors of measurement. (Chapter 7 in Paraskevopoulos and Kirk is helpful in interpreting such differences.)

Q: *May one extract just the subtests in the areas in which the child is having problems?*

A: It is possible to extract specific subtests for specific purposes. Particularly with older children, where the test as a whole would not be appropriate, you may wish to administer specific subtests. If in the light of other diagnostic information you are certain that the child has difficulty in only one or two specific functions, you may wish to get an estimate of how the child stacks up against a group of normally progressing children of his age. Or you may wish to reinforce informal observations. If you are only interested in finding out if the child can understand the English language, you may wish to give him the Auditory Reception test. If you are interested only in his ability to express himself, you may wish to give him the Verbal Expression test and perhaps the Grammatic Closure test.

Q: *In giving the ITPA, is the examiner restricted to following the time limits recommended, or can the child be allowed more time?*

A: For the test as a whole, the time of one hour is not a rigid limit. The time needed is dependent on the examiner's facility in administering the test and on the responses of the child. New examiners often run over the one hour, and if much more than that is needed, two sittings are usually advisable.

The child's responses are not timed except on the Visual Closure subtest, where the child's response coincides with the thirty seconds allowed for the presentation. The one-minute time suggested for the Verbal Expression subtest is only approximate and only indicative of what might be expected.

Q: *If a youngster has just passed his sixth birthday but is suspected from teacher reports and other test results to be performing below average, is it permissible to begin testing with Demo I instead of Demo II?*

A: Yes. We *do* begin at a lower level (that is, a slow six-year-old or a retarded seven- or eight-year-old might begin with Demo I instead of Demo II). Similarly, a bright five-year-old might begin with Demo II instead of Demo I.

Q: *I have made my own tape recording of the Sound Blending, Auditory Closure, Grammatic Closure, and Auditory Sequential Memory subtests. Is it valid to present the tests in this manner?*

A: No, for three reasons. In the first place, the test was not standardized with tape recordings. As with any standardized test, if you are going to use the standardized norms it is most important to follow standardized procedure in administering the test. Second, it is questionable whether the tape can hold the attention of young children as well as an alert, adaptable examiner can. Although some older children are fascinated with the mechanics of it, it is dehumanizing for others. Third, it does not allow for a presentation of necessary repeats and adaptations or for smooth transition from one part to another.

Q: *On some of the subtests the wording gets rather monotonous when used for every item. Is it permissible to drop out some of the wording after the pattern of response has been well established?*

A: Usually not, but with older children it is sometimes permissible to omit "Listen" on the later items of the Auditory Sequential Memory test and "which one of these" on the Visual Association test. On the Visual Sequential Memory test the wording *must be exact,* else the child's time for looking at the sequence will vary.

Q: *If one subtest is invalidated because of unforeseen problems, what do you use for a reference point (mean scaled score)?*

A: In such a situation the raw scores of the other nine subtests should be used to determine a mean scaled score (SS), dividing the sum of the nine scaled scores by nine.

Q: *Why, if you profile by age score, is the profile more severe than when it is profiled by SS?*

A: The more extreme variations are due to a difference between the two scales (age scores and scaled scores) on which the profiles are made. In an effort to put both kinds of data on one page of the Record Form, the scale intervals between age scores are greater than those between comparable scaled scores. This makes the differences appear greater. The effect can be shown graphically by the contrasting profiles of the identical scaled scores presented in Figure 2. Because the scores in the left-hand profile were plotted on a broader scale, the differences appear more extreme.

Figure 2. Contrasting Score Profiles Resulting from Different Scales

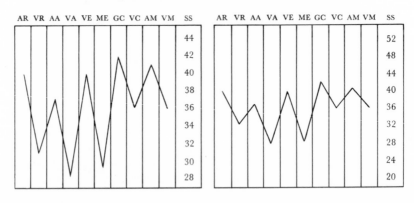

Q: *Why are the deviations between scaled scores and age scores different on different subtests?*

A: Within any set of standardization data the range of scores varies from subgroup to subgroup and from age group to age group. The norms for age scores do not take this variability into account, whereas scaled scores are a statistical measure which deals with this factor. Age scores, therefore, do not give a complete representation of where the child stands in relation to the standardization group, whereas the scaled scores show more realistically how a child compares to the normative group. This difference is demonstrated in Figure 3, which shows the scores on two tests with differing ranges. On Test A the age scores ranged from 4-10 to 7-2; on Test B they ranged from 5-4 to 6-10. A score on Test B equivalent to age 5-4 is the very lowest in the group, whereas a score equivalent to age 5-4 on Test A is not so extreme in relation to the rest of the group. The corresponding scaled score would be lower for a child who scores at 5-4 on Test B than for one who scores at 5-4 on Test A.

Figure 3. Variations in Age Score Ranges on Two Different Tests

Test A	Age Scores	Test B
•	7-2	
•	7-0	
• •	6-10	•
• •	6-8	• • •
• • •	6-6	• •
• • • •	6-4	• • • • •
• • • •	6-2	• • • • •
• • • • • • •	6-0	• • • • • •
• • •	5-10	• • • • •
` • •	5-8	• • •
•	5-6	• • •
•	5-4	•
•	5-2	
• •	5-0	
•	4-10	

Q: *Who is qualified to administer the ITPA? Is it restricted to psychologists?*

A: The ITPA was developed as a diagnostic tool, and its authors believe that diagnosis should lead to suggestions for remediation. It is not merely a classification test to determine general intelligence, as are the Binet and the WISC, which are used primarily for labelling or placement of children in special groups. Therefore, the ITPA should be made available to those who can and will use it to produce remedial efforts. Just as a diagnostic reading test is most effectively used by the reading specialist, so the ITPA is most effectively used by the properly trained psychologist, school counselor, diagnostic remedial teacher, or speech correctionist. The field of employment does not determine who is properly trained. Any of the above specialists who have had adequate training in the administration of individual tests and who are willing to study the ITPA and demonstrate facility in its administration and application should be competent to use the test.

Proper use of the ITPA, however, is not acquired lightly. It is not a test that is glanced over a couple of times and then administered — no matter how many other tests the individual may be familiar with. Its administration is rather rigidly defined and requires careful study and usually some supervision. To this end, workshops for small groups of individuals who wish to acquire proficiency in the administration of the ITPA have been organized. For more information about the workshops, write the University of Illinois Press.

Q: *If, during testing, a child is accidentally presented with an item above his final ceiling, why is he not given credit for that item?*

A: Basically, because that is not the way the norms were established. The fifty items of the test were arranged in order of difficulty with slight modification to assure that no more than three consecutive items called for the same response and that "yes-no" alternation was not present. A more rigid ceiling (such as three consecutive failures) would extend the test too far, since it is difficult to obtain three consecutive errors when there is a fifty-fifty chance of success as there is with yes/no answers. On the other hand, it was found from statistical evidence that a more lenient ceiling than three out of seven would have lowered the reliability.

Q: *If an examiner inadvertently goes down farther than necessary to obtain a basal and the child fails an item below five consecutive successes, is it necessary to get a new basal below that failure?*

A: No. Disregard the failure.

QUESTIONS ABOUT THE SUBTESTS

Auditory Reception

Q: *I find that at some point many children tend to give all "yes" or all "no" answers. Can this be avoided?*

A: Probably not. When a young child approaches his ceiling he often answers in that way. It is important, especially as the child reaches the limit of his ability, to maintain his interest and attention by a pause or an enthusiastic "Listen, John. Do zebras burrow?" Do not make a marked change of pace in stating the item, but speak at a moderate rate.

Q: *Some children are afraid to make a mistake and therefore answer "I don't know" to many questions. Are these responses scored as failures?*

A: It is quite permissible to encourage a child with "Try it," or "What do you think, do ants crawl?" or (if necessary) "Make a guess." With such a child you may want to say, "You won't get them *all* right, but try them anyway." Do try to get a response from him. If you cannot entice him to answer, score the item as a failure.

Visual Reception

Q: *What do you say on a Visual Reception test item when the child says, "There isn't any"?*

A: You may flip back to the stimulus picture (if you have not previously done so on this item), saying, "Let's look again. See this?" Then, reexposing the alternative pictures, repeat, "Find one here." If he still refuses to make a choice, say, "Choose one you think it might be."

Q: *How does it happen that a child sometimes receives a low score on the Visual Reception subtest and a high score on the Visual Association subtest?*

A: This sometimes happens because of poor administration, poor scoring, or test fallibility. If the Auditory Reception or Visual Reception test is more than two or three years lower than the comparable association test, and if no errors are found in the administration and scoring, the test might be repeated a week later.

Remember that an effort was made to limit the task on each subtest to the function under consideration and keep other requirements at least two years below the level of that required for the function being tested. In the Auditory Association test, for example, the vocabulary and word usage were kept at a lower level than the concepts of relationship involved. Instead of saying, "A cube is square; a sphere is ————," Item 17 says, "A block is square; a ball is ————." The test is not infallible, however, and once in a while such vagaries do occur. If it were not so, the statistical reliabilities would be higher. When a marked deviation occurs, the scoring and administration should be very carefully checked.

Visual Association

Q: *On the Visual Association subtest, if a six-year-old child begins with Demo I and Item 1 instead of Demo I and Item 11 and then fails some items below Item 11, although he passes 11 through 14, how is his test scored? All the other subtests were begun at Demo II.*

A: The lower failures should *not* be disregarded in this case because the examiner cannot be sure that Items 11 through 14 would have been answered successfully if the child had not had the practice in Items 1 through 10.

Q: *On the Visual Association test is it necessary to repeat all of the words: "What goes with this? Which one of these? This one, or this one, or this one?"*

A: No, only "What goes with this? Which one of these?" (as the examiner gestures in a circular movement). For younger or distractable children the examiner may add: "This one, or this one, or this one, or this one?"

Q: *On Item 11 of the Visual Association subtest many children choose the parachute instead of the space capsule. Since children also see parachutes used in the recovery of space capsules on TV, why is this not the creditable answer?*

A: Not only is the spaceman more specifically associated with the space capsule than with the parachute, but the item analysis also indicated that the space capsule gave a better age differentiation to the norms.

Q: *In administering the Visual Association subtest is it permissible to label an item for the child?*

A: Yes, on the demonstration items only, if the child requests it or if he seems puzzled. Verbalizing on the test items makes it possible for the child to make associations on a verbal basis.

Q: *What does the examiner do on the Visual Association subtest when the child verbally labels the answer instead of pointing?*

A: Since verbalizing helps to cover up any weakness in the visual channel, it is necessary to tell the child early in the game, "Don't tell me; just show me." This is more emphatic than saying, "You don't have to tell me," and usually the verbalizing response will drop out after a few reminders.

Verbal Expression

(See Section IV for discussion of scoring problems.)

Q: *Some children are very reticent and need a great deal of urging to get them to respond. How much can they be encouraged?*

A: On page 49 of the *Examiner's Manual* the statement is made, "a maximum of 5 encouragements may be useful." It is also helpful to get in the habit of recording an *E* every time you do ask the child, "Tell me something else." Such encouragement should be used only when the child pauses or hesitates between responses or seems reluctant to talk. A questioning or expectant look on the part of the examiner during a pause may be sufficient to draw out additional responses without giving the child a feeling he is being prodded.

Q: *On the Verbal Expression test is it true that no more than ten points may be credited in any one category?*

A: No. There is no restriction on the number of credits in any one category.

Q: *What is the significance of the absence of labels in the Verbal Expression subtest?*

A: Older children are less apt to give such an unsophisticated response as "This is a button." This is why (*in this one category only*) credit is given if the child uses a label after questioning or in an otherwise irrelevant response such as, "My baby brother has a big blue ball."

Q: *A child can get a good score on the Verbal Expression subtest and still not use good syntax. Is this an accurate indicator of how well he expresses himself?*

A: Nicety of expression, proper grammar, and good syntax are not always indicative of good verbal expression. This test disregards the automatically learned use of grammatic rules because we are trying to measure how many ideas the child puts into verbal form. As long as he can get an idea across to another person, he is communicating, even though it is not in good grammatic form. On the other hand, you can string a lot of words together in beautiful syntax and still not really say anything. The Grammatic Closure subtest attempts to measure the use of proper word forms and idioms.

Q: *What do you do in giving the Verbal Expression subtest when a youngster keeps drawing comparisons with other objects; for example, "the block is shaped like dice . . . like a cube of ice . . . like a big box . . . like a house with no roof," etc.?*

A. When a child shows perseveration in this manner, giving a chain of responses based on one idea, it is permissible for the examiner to say, "You told me what it is shaped like. Now tell me something else." The above responses would not receive more than one point for comparison, since they are all based on the shape of the block. If the child had based some comparisons on color, composition, or some other function or characteristic, he could also have received further credit for that comparison. One should therefore not intervene in a child's spontaneous response except where such chaining is obvious. See page 54 of the *Examiner's Manual.*

Manual Expression

Q: *In scoring Item 10 (eggbeater) on the Manual Expression subtest, where do you draw the line in determining if the hand holding the eggbeater is "above the rotating hand?"*

A: If the hand that is holding the eggbeater is above the *center of rotation* of the rotating hand, credit is allowed for point *e.*

Q: *On the Manual Expression subtest can you give credit for Item 7 if the child pretends his finger is the pencil and points it toward the rotating hand?*

A: Yes, any clear method of pretending to hold a pencil in the pencil sharpener is acceptable.

Q: *In the Manual Expression subtest many children demonstrate carrying the suitcase. Why is this not given credit?*

A: Because this response was found to lower the age discrimination of the subtest. Young children tended to make this response, whereas older children did not. Therefore it would have been misleading to give credit for this response.

Q: *On the Manual Expression subtest, if a child does not want to demonstrate what we do with a cigarette and matches, what does the examiner do?*

A: Recent publicity of smoking hazards has occasionally developed some hesitancy on this item, but usually the child can be encouraged to attempt it if the examiner recognizes and verbalizes the child's concern. It should be recognized that for nearly every item there are some children who will not or cannot demonstrate the concept, and the examiner must be careful not to read his own prejudices into such a failure. For cases in which it is necessary to eliminate this item, new norms are available. These are presented in Appendix B.

Q: *In the Motor Expression subtest in the Experimental Edition of the ITPA credit was allowed for "substitute gestures" on many items. In the Revised Edition substitute gestures are specifically permitted for the camera, for the suitcase, and for the pencil sharpener. Is it permissible to give credit for the telephone if the child pretends to punch buttons as on a touch-tone telephone?*

A: Yes. Touch-tone telephones were rare at the time the test was published. If the child were blind or very low in visual reception he would have to depend on the verbal stimulus, "Show me what we do with a telephone." Therefore he should be given credit for the substitute gesture.

Grammatic Closure
(See Section V.)

Q: *How do you score "... he has stolen" on Item 27 of the Grammatic Closure subtest?*

A: This is scored as correct since "... he has written" is scored correct on Item 9. The scoring of these two items may make you very uncomfortable and is not completely satisfactory however it is done.

Basically, on this test we did not give credit unless the child indicated his ability to use a particular form of the word. The child who is not sure of this form often evades the issue by repeating the form presented.

Visual Closure

Q: *Must the five Visual Closure test items be given in order or may they be scattered throughout the testing time?*

A: As with any test, they must be given in sequence, since they were standardized in that fashion.

Auditory Sequential Memory

Q: *In presenting the bracketed pair of items in the Auditory Sequential Memory test, does the tester present both pairs of the set if the first pair is repeated incorrectly?*

A: *All* items are presented in the prescribed sequence until a basal and a ceiling are obtained. In sampling, present item pairs 1 *and* 2, 3 *and* 4, 6 *and* 7, and so on, until the first failure occurs. If this failure occurs on the first item of a starred pair, sampling is immediately discontinued, the basal is obtained, and then, returning to the point of first failure, the second item of the starred pair is presented if further testing is necessary to reach a ceiling. In item-by-item progression without sampling (for children under four years) present each item in sequence, ignoring the stars, until a ceiling is reached.

Visual Sequential Memory
(See Section III.)

Q: *When a child fails Demo II on the first trial, shouldn't the next item for obtaining a basal be Item 3 (instead of Demo I as indicated)?*

A: Demo II is always given before Items 4, 5, and so on. Therefore, it is never given in backward progression when seeking a basal. When a six-year-old begins with Demo II, he goes either to Item 5 (after he understands the task) or to Demo I (if he fails to understand the task on Demo II). This is why the notations on the card refer you to Demo I if Demo II is failed after adequate tutelage.

For the child below 6-0 who begins with Demo I, Demo II is presented after Item 2 (or 3, as the case may be). If he then does not understand the task on Demo II with adequate tutelage he is functioning like a child below four years of age and should proceed backward through Item 1. Then, if a ceiling has not been reached, Demo II should be repeated and forward progression resumed, item by item, until a ceiling is reached. Demonstration items are never scored and are never included in figuring ceilings or basals.

Q: *When Demo I has been given, why is Demo II necessary, since no credit is given?*

A: Demo II is given at the appropriate time to make sure that younger children understand the task.

Q: *On the Visual Sequential Memory subtest, is it necessary to have two consecutive errors above any failure on the highest sampling error, or can complete failure on a sampling item be included in the two consecutive failures?*

A: Complete failure on a sampling item may be included in the two consecutive failures needed to reach a ceiling. If a child fails both trials of a sampling item and then fails the next easier item completely, his ceiling has been achieved.

Q: *When a second trial is necessary on any item of the Visual Sequential Memory subtest, is it necessary to repeat all of the initial directions?*

A: Yes. When the child makes a mistake on the first trial, the examiner says, "Not quite," as he shuffles the chips; then, as he presents the sequence, he says, "Now look again — this one here and this one here and this one here" (or, "Now look again — take a good look so you can make it," as the case may be).

Q: *There are times that I would prefer to give the Visual Sequential Memory subtest without using the sampling procedure. Does this make a difference or affect the child's score?*

A: The sampling procedure serves to quickly determine the child's appropriate level of ability so that the whole test will not have to be administered. If the child is capable of reproducing six-figure sequences, it would be a long and tiresome procedure to have him reproduce all of the three-figure, four-figure, and five-figure sequences before he reaches the level of six figures. Until further research is done, and perhaps new norms established, to determine the effect of *not* sampling, the test should be presented as it was standardized.

Sound Blending
(See Section VI.)

Q: *On Section A of the Sound Blending subtest what do you do if the child just points to the picture without naming it?*

A: As on the demonstration item, if the child does not respond *verbally* the examiner points to the picture the child has just pointed to and says, "What *is* that?" If he does not respond at all, the examiner repeats, "Which one am I talking about?"

Q: *On the Sound Blending subtest, why is it necessary to give all of Section A?*

A: The basal was very lenient on this section because we wanted to extend the test of sound blending ability to very young children, whom other sound blending tests do not include. Some young children will "catch on" at the last minute and then go on to Section B. Unless the child fails completely at this level, he is given Section B, which is where most sound blending tests begin.

Q: *Why is the pyscholinguistic age norm ceiling at 8-7 for the Sound Blending test?*

A: Because this test represents an ability which is usually acquired by eight or nine years of age, especially by the average child represented in the standardization sample.

QUESTIONS ABOUT THE INTERPRETATION OF SCORES

Q: (a) *What is the validity of the scores obtained on the ITPA for children above ten years of age?* (b) *How can the ITPA be used to diagnose learning disabilities in high school? Don't beg the question by talking about getting to these children earlier. We can't shoot those who escape notice at a younger age!*

A: The ITPA is not all things to all children. It was specifically devised to assess certain relevant abilities among children of about three to nine years of age. The norms extend from two to ten years, but at both extremes the norms are quite gross. Clinically, some use of the test beyond these limits may be made under certain circumstances and with certain precautions:

1. Intraindividual comparisons may be made between subtest psycholinguistic age (PLA) scores if they do not exceed the ceiling. If a child reaches the ceiling or falls below the norms on any subtest, one does not know his ability in that area.

2. You cannot use the chronological age (CA) to determine scaled scores for children above CA 10-3, since there are no norms for CAs above that age limit. Neither should scaled scores be derived or extrapolated from the highest CA norms.

3. However, if a child whose CA is above 10-3 and whose PLA is below 10-3 does not exceed the ceiling on any of the subtests,

very limited use may be made of scaled scores derived by using the PLA in place of the CA in Table 2. All such scores will be deceptively high and should be used only to determine the significance of differences between the child's own scores.

4. For children above ten years who are not suspected of mental retardation but who appear to be deficient in specific areas, selective subtests may be administered to verify clinical suspicions. For example, a junior high child with a language problem and a history of speech difficulty may have a deficit in making use of the redundancies of his experiences in language, in perceptual closure, or perhaps in auditory memory. You may want to give him the tests that would confirm or negate your clinical impression.

5. For reading-disabled children, one may want to know the child's abilities or disabilities in areas closely related to reading disability, such as sequential memory, closure, or auditory association.

Q: *Can you use the ITPA with trainable mentally retarded children?*

A: Yes, although you may want to use the norms somewhat differently. Since the ITPA is an intraindividual test which attempts to compare the child's own abilities and disabilities, we consider such use appropriate for trainable mentally retarded children. Age scores may be more appropriate here, since some problems arise in using scaled scores.

Q: *Do norms on subtests vary extensively with nonwhite subjects?*

A: Studies on the ITPA with blacks, Indians, and Mexican-Americans show that the functioning of minority groups may be related more to culture than to race, except for auditory and sequential memory. Middle-class blacks, for example, score similarly to middle-class whites except for the superiority of the blacks in auditory sequential memory. Indians and Mexican-Americans seem to be superior to whites and blacks in visual sequential memory (see Kirk, 1972).

Q: *How much of a deviation in age scores is indicative of a disability?*

A: This depends upon several considerations, among which are: (a) statistical factors involved, (b) the pattern of deficits, and (c) the age of the child.

(a) As explained earlier (page 72), a child may have a more serious deficit on one test than on another and still not show as much deviation in age scores on that test as on the other. This is why the scaled score is a more reliable measure of disability. Use of the standard error of measurement is valuable here (see Para-skevopoulos and Kirk, ch. 7).

(b) The amount of deviation should also be viewed in relation to the pattern of deficits. A smaller difference might be considered substantial if it occurs in conjunction with other deficits in the same channel (or level or process).

(c) The age of the child should also be considered. This is of first importance, since a two-year deviation in the scores of a four-year-old child is more serious than a two-year deviation in the scores of an eight-year-old child.

Chapters 7 and 8 of Paraskevopoulos and Kirk give a more complete answer to this question. The most statistically reliable method of determining whether the difference between two scores is really significant is found in Chapter 7 of Paraskevopoulos and Kirk. By using Table 7-10 and either Table 7-7, 7-8, or 7-9 (depending on the kind of scores you are dealing with) you can determine with statistical accuracy whether or not there is a "true" difference between two test scores.

Q: *At what age can diagnostic testing or observation be profitably begun?*

A: The earlier the better. Some observations are meaningful before testing is feasible. For example, the two-year-old who has no interest in appropriate pictures may be slow in gaining meaning from two-dimensional representations such as pictures.

Children below two and one-half years of age are often quite difficult to test in a standardized manner, especially by a stranger. It is very important to make contact before the testing is begun. Informal activities which require imitation and following directions should be utilized first. This may require successive contacts with the child.

Q: *Where would you draw the line in defining the child with a learning disability and a mentally retarded child?*

A: The question of labelling these children as mentally retarded or learning disabled is not the major issue. The important thing to know is what kind of an educational program is needed for each child. (See Kirk and Kirk [1971], p. 119 ff.)

The typically mentally retarded child shows insignificant deviations among subtest scores but has a mean scaled score well below normal.

The child with learning disabilities shows substantial deviations among his abilities and his disabilities as indicated by his subtest scores on the ITPA and on other diagnostic instruments. In some areas the child will be performing at a normal level or beyond. Many of these children are found sitting in classes for the mentally retarded — misdiagnosed and untreated.

It is possible, of course, to have a mentally retarded child who is also learning disabled, that is, who shows a low mean scaled score and also substantial deviations in ability with few, if any, abilities scoring at a normal level. If many of his abilities score at or above average for his age, he is probably a learning disabled child.

Q: *In many items it would appear that more than one answer should be correct. How were correct responses determined?*

A: Face validity was evaluated first. Later the item analysis provided information on homogeneity and age differentiation. The percentage of children passing at each age level (difficulty level) and the correlation of each item with the total score (discriminatory power) were the primary criteria for final item selection. (See Paraskevopoulos and Kirk.)

Q: *What are the standard errors of the psycholinguistic ages?*

A: See Paraskevopoulos and Kirk, p. 115.

Q: *Can the psycholinguistic quotient (PLQ) be used in place of an IQ in estimating the overall ability of a child?*

A: There is some evidence that the psycholinguistic quotient (psycholinguistic age divided by chronological age) is quite comparable to a Stanford-Binet IQ. Although this was not the initial purpose in developing the ITPA, at least one study of first-grade children indicates a correlation of 0.90 between the Binet IQ and the PLQ (Huizinga, 1973).

Q: *How do you figure the CA for use with the ITPA?*

A: We figure the CA to the closest month. If a child is five years, three months, and fifteen days, we give him a CA of 5-3. If he is five years, three months, and sixteen days, we give him a CA of 5-4. This is the method used with the Stanford-Binet rather than that used with the WISC.

Q: *How much is considered a substantial difference between the CA and the PLA?*

A: The composite PLA is used in much the same way as is a mental age (MA). It has limited use except for classification purposes, and the amount of discrepancy considered substantial depends upon your purpose. It is a global score indicative of the level of psycholinguistic (and perhaps intellectual) development. The PLA on individual subtests may be of service in selecting and developing materials for the child in the same way that an MA would be. It is also used for comparative purposes with other tests which are expressed in age scores. It indicates the *level* at which a child is functioning in that particular area, but significant discrepancies are more accurately determined by the scaled scores.

Q: *What are the remedial methods for the ITPA?*

A: There are on the market several programs of materials and suggestions which can be used at the discretion of the teacher. Any such materials, however, must be evaluated carefully for the appropriateness in each case. There are two such programs which have recently come on the market and which are based on the model of the ITPA: Karnes (1972) and Minskoff, Wiseman, and Minskoff (1973). Some suggestions may also be obtained from Kirk and Kirk (1971).

Appendix A

A Record Form for
the Observation of ITPA Administration

After you have carefully studied the *Examiner's Manual,* practiced the test by yourself, and attempted to give it five or six times, you should examine a child in the presence of an experienced and well-trained ITPA examiner. It is recommended that you be examined at this early stage so that you not continue to practice any errors you may be making. After you have developed greater facility with the test you should be observed again. The accompanying record form might be used by the observer to note those areas in which you are doing well and those areas in which you need further efficiency or improved performance. This observation is crucial in learning to give the test well.

The Record Form for the Observation of ITPA Administration lists ten critical procedures for good test administration along the left side of the chart. Across the top are listed the twelve subtests of the battery. Critical procedures which are not applicable to particular subtests are blocked out. The observer should note in each open block whether or not you have adequately handled that testing procedure for that particular subtest. The observer should also make notes at the bottom or on the back of the sheet so that any problems can be discussed with you at the end of the test.

It is important that the observer note the following:

1. *Efficiency.* Did the examiner appear to be familiar with the materials, where they were located, which ones were appropriate for the upcoming test? Did he waste time between tests because he was not quite sure which test and which materials were next?

2. *Demonstration.* Were the demonstration items administered as prescribed in the *Examiner's Manual?* Did the child understand the task? If not, did the examiner use other means to clarify the task to the child? Did he then return to the prescribed form before proceeding to the test items? Did he confirm or correct the child's responses?

3. *Basal.* Was the basal established before proceeding with the rest of the subtest? Did the examiner overtest?

87

4. *Ceiling.* Did the examiner know when the ceiling was achieved, or did he give unnecessary items?

5. *Repetition of items.* Did he make proper use of a second trial where appropriate and only where appropriate? Did he question adequately on Verbal Expression? Did he handle negations properly on Auditory Association? On the Grammatic Closure test did he repeat the item when (and only when) no form of the anticipated word was used? Did he use second trials properly on the Sequential Memory tests? On Auditory Closure? Was he careful not to repeat items on Sound Blending?

6. *Timing.* Was the half-second interval followed in presenting the digits? The Sound Blending phonemes? Was the exposure time accurate in the Visual Sequential Memory and Visual Closure tests? Was the Verbal Expression test given adequate timing without cutting off responses which were relevant, discrete, and factual?

7. *Wording.* Was the wording of the directions followed exactly? Did the examiner use a conversational tone, or was he stilted and unnatural? Was his speech too rapid or too slow?

8. *Recording.* Was the examiner familiar with the record form? Did he use it inconspicuously and easily? Did he record in such a way that another person could score it?

9. *Scoring.* Was the examiner familiar with scoring standards so that he did not have to hesitate on such subtests as the Auditory Association, the Grammatic Closure, and the Manual Expression subtests? Did he know when to question on the Verbal Expression subtest?

10. *Sampling procedure.* Did he make proper use of the sampling procedure on the two tests where it is applicable?

A careful study of these points and a self-evaluation based on them will greatly facilitate proficiency in the administration of the test. Critical observation by a knowledgeable person will be very helpful. Often it is more valuable to have the observer act as the child, in order to present responses which test your understanding of the above points, than it is to have a child who may or may not provide problems in administration. If the observer does act as the child, however, his emphasis should be on providing critical problems in procedure rather than on misbehavior and bizarre responses.

RECORD FORM
FOR THE OBSERVATION
OF ITPA ADMINISTRATION

ITPA Subtests

Critical Procedures to Evaluate	Auditory Reception	Visual Reception	Visual Sequential Memory	Auditory Association	Auditory Sequential Memory	Visual Association	Visual Closure	Verbal Expression	Grammatic Closure	Manual Expression	Auditory Closure	Sound Blending
Efficiency												
Demonstration												
Basal							▨	▨	▨	▨		
Ceiling							▨	▨		▨		
Repetition of items*												
Timing	▨			▨	▨					▨		
Wording**												
Recording												
Scoring												
Sampling	▨	▨		▨		▨	▨	▨	▨	▨	▨	▨

* Including questioning to clarify responses.
** Including presentation of the Sound Blending test.

OTHER REMARKS:

Appendix B

Norms for Eliminating Item 6
of the Manual Expression Subtest

Some examiners have objected to Item 6 in the Manual Expression subtest, which involves demonstrating the use of a cigarette and matches. Our experience has indicated that scarcely one or two children out of a hundred refuse to attempt this item, saying, "Smoking is bad," or, "You're not supposed to smoke." Usually you can persuade them to attempt the item by saying, "Yes, smoking is bad, but show me how some people do it." For those few examiners who wish to delete this item, the accompanying Table 4 and Table 5 are provided.

It should be pointed out that out of a large number of items explored, this item was selected because of its reliability and its age discrimination. The reliability of the norms in Tables 4 and 5 is not known, and the complete subtest should be given if possible.

Table 4 presents adjusted scaled scores developed from the raw scores of the normative group when the scores on Item 6 were omitted. In the extreme left-hand and extreme right-hand columns are presented the raw scores omitting Item 6. In the other columns are presented the corresponding scaled scores of each age interval. When Item 6 is omitted, these columns may take the place of the corresponding Manual Expression columns in *Examiner's Manual* Table 2. To find the scaled scores for manual expression under these circumstances: (a) find the given raw score in the left-hand column and (b) read across to the appropriate age column to find the corresponding scaled score. Scaled scores for other subtests, of course, are obtained in the usual manner from the norms in the *Examiner's Manual* Table 2.

Table 5 presents adjusted PLA scores to be used when Item 6 is omitted. The subtest PLA scores in the left-hand part of the table are substituted for the Manual Expression column in *Examiner's Manual* Table 1. This presents the age score corresponding to each raw score.

The composite PLA scores in the right-hand section of Table 5 are to be used instead of the *Examiner's Manual* Table 3 if Item 6 has been eliminated.

TABLE 4. ADJUSTED SCALED SCORES FOR ELIMINATION OF ITEM 6 IN MANUAL EXPRESSION SUBTEST (for Examiner's Manual Table 2)

Age Groups

Raw Scores	2-4 to 2-7	2-8 to 2-11	3-0 to 3-3	3-4 to 3-7	3-8 to 3-11	4-0 to 4-3	4-4 to 4-7	4-8 to 4-11	5-0 to 5-3	5-4 to 5-7	5-8 to 5-11	6-0 to 6-3	6-4 to 6-7	6-8 to 6-11	7-0 to 7-3	7-4 to 7-7	7-8 to 7-11	8-0 to 8-3	8-4 to 8-7	8-8 to 8-11	9-0 to 9-3	9-4 to 9-7	9-8 to 9-11	10-0 to 10-3	Raw Scores
0	31	30	28	27	25	23	22	21	20	18	16	14	13	12	10	8	6	5	3	2	2	2	2	2	0
1	32	31	30	28	26	24	23	22	22	19	17	16	14	13	11	9	7	6	4	3	3	3	3	3	1
2	34	33	31	30	28	25	24	23	23	20	18	17	15	14	12	10	8	7	5	5	4	4	4	4	2
3	35	34	32	31	29	26	25	24	24	21	19	18	16	16	13	11	9	8	7	6	6	6	6	6	3
4	37	35	33	32	30	27	26	25	25	22	20	19	18	17	15	12	10	10	8	7	7	7	7	7	4
5	38	36	34	33	31	28	27	26	26	23	21	20	19	18	16	14	12	11	9	8	8	8	8	8	5
6	40	38	35	35	32	30	28	27	27	24	22	21	20	19	17	15	13	12	10	9	9	9	9	9	6
7	41	39	37	36	33	32	29	28	28	25	23	22	21	20	18	16	14	13	11	11	10	10	10	10	7
8	43	41	38	37	34	33	30	29	29	26	24	23	22	21	19	17	15	15	12	12	12	12	12	12	8
9	44	43	39	38	36	34	32	30	30	27	25	25	23	22	20	18	16	16	13	13	13	13	13	13	9
10	46	45	40	39	37	35	33	31	31	29	27	26	24	24	21	19	18	17	14	14	14	14	14	14	10
11	48	46	41	40	38	36	34	32	32	30	28	27	25	25	22	20	19	18	15	15	15	15	15	15	11
12	49	48	42	41	39	37	36	33	33	31	29	28	27	26	23	21	20	19	17	17	16	16	16	16	12
13	50	49	43	43	40	38	37	34	34	32	30	29	28	27	24	22	21	20	18	18	18	18	18	18	13
14	51	50	44	44	41	39	38	35	35	33	31	30	29	28	25	23	22	21	19	19	19	19	19	19	14
15	52	51	45	45	42	40	39	36	36	34	32	31	30	29	26	24	23	22	20	20	20	20	20	20	15
16	54	53	46	46	43	42	40	37	37	35	33	32	31	30	27	25	24	23	22	21	21	21	21	21	16
17	55	54	48	47	45	43	41	38	38	36	34	33	32	31	28	27	25	25	23	22	22	22	22	22	17
18	57	55	49	48	46	44	42	39	39	37	35	34	33	32	29	28	26	26	24	23	23	23	23	23	18
19	58	57	51	49	47	45	43	40	40	38	36	35	34	33	31	29	27	27	25	24	24	24	24	24	19
20	60	58	52	51	48	46	44	41	41	39	37	36	35	34	33	30	29	28	27	26	25	25	25	25	20
21	61	59	53	52	49	47	45	42	42	40	38	37	36	35	34	31	30	29	28	27	27	27	27	27	21
22	62	61	54	53	50	48	46	43	43	41	39	38	37	36	35	33	31	30	29	28	28	28	28	28	22
23	64	63	55	54	51	49	47	44	44	42	40	39	38	37	36	34	32	31	30	29	29	29	29	29	23
24	65	64	57	55	52	50	48	45	45	43	41	40	39	38	37	35	33	32	32	31	30	30	30	30	24
25	66	66	58	56	53	51	49	46	46	44	42	41	40	39	38	36	34	34	33	32	31	31	31	31	25
26	68	67	59	58	54	52	50	47	47	45	43	42	41	40	39	37	35	35	34	33	32	32	32	32	26
27		68	60	59	56	53	51	48	48	46	44	43	42	41	40	38	36	36	35	34	33	33	33	33	27
28			61	60	57	54	52	49	49	47	45	44	43	42	41	39	38	38	37	36	35	35	35	35	28
29			63	61	58	55	53	50	50	48	46	45	44	43	42	40	40	39	38	37	36	36	36	36	29
30			64	62	59	56	54	51	51	49	47	46	45	44	43	41	41	40	39	38	37	37	37	37	30
31			65	63	60	57	55	52	52	50	48	47	46	45	44	42	42	42	40	39	38	38	38	38	31
32			66	64	61	58	56	53	53	51	49	48	47	46	45	43	43	43	41	40	39	39	39	39	32
33				65	62	59	57	54	54	52	50	49	48	47	46	44	45	44	43	42	42	41	41	40	33
34				66	63	60	58	55	55	53	51	50	49	48	47	45	46	45	44	43	43	42	42	41	34
35				67	64	62	59	56	56	54	52	52	51	49	48	48	47	46	45	44	44	43	43	43	35
36				68	65	63	60	57	57	55	53	53	52	50	49	49	48	48	46	45	45	45	45	44	36

TABLE 5. ADJUSTED PLA SCORES FOR ELIMINATION OF ITEM 6
IN MANUAL EXPRESSION SUBTEST

(for *Examiner's* Manual Table 1) Subtest PLA		(for *Examiner's Manual* Table 3) Composite PLA					
Raw Score	PLA	Sum of Scores (Interval)	PLA	Sum of Scores (Interval)	PLA	Sum of Scores (Interval)	PLA
0		7–9	2–0	134–137	4–9	249–250	7–5
1		10–12	2–1	138–142	4–10	251–253	7–6
2		13–16	2–2	143–146	4–11	254–256	7–7
3	2–2	17–20	2–3	147–150	5–0	257–258	7–8
4	2–4	21–24	2–4	151–154	5–1	259–261	7–9
5	2–6	25–28	2–5	155–158	5–2	262–265	7–10
6	2–8	29–32	2–6	159–162	5–3	266–269	7–11
7	2–10	33–36	2–7	163–166	5–4	270–272	8–0
8	3–0	37–40	2–8	167–170	5–5	273–274	8–1
9	3–2	41–43	2–9	171–174	5–6	275–276	8–2
10	3–4	44–47	2–10	175–178	5–7	277–278	8–3
11	3–6	48–50	2–11	179–182	5–8	279–280	8–4
12	3–8	51–54	3–0	183–186	5–9	281–283	8–5
13	3–10	55–58	3–1	187–189	5–10	284–285	8–6
14	4–1	59–62	3–2	190–192	5–11	286–288	8–7
15	4–4	63–66	3–3	193–196	6–0	289–290	8–8
16	4–8	67–70	3–4	197–199	6–1	291–292	8–9
17	4–11	71–74	3–5	200–202	6–2	293–294	8–10
18	5–2	75–78	3–6	203–206	6–3	295–296	8–11
19	5–5	79–82	3–7	207–209	6–4	297–298	9–0
20	5–9	83–86	3–8	210–213	6–5	299–300	9–1
21	6–1	87–90	3–9	214–216	6–6	301–302	9–2
22	6–5	91–94	3–10	217–220	6–7	303–304	9–3
23	6–8	95–98	3–11	221–224	6–8	305	9–4
24	7–1	99–102	4–0	225–228	6–9	306–307	9–5
25	7–5	103–105	4–1	229–231	6–10	308–309	9–6
26	7–10	106–109	4–2	232–233	6–11	310–311	9–7
27	8–3	110–113	4–3	234–236	7–0	312	9–8
28	8–7	114–117	4–4	237–239	7–1	313–314	9–9
29	9–1	118–121	4–5	240–243	7–2	315–316	9–10
30	9–8	122–125	4–6	244–246	7–3	317	9–11
31	10–3	126–129	4–7	247–248	7–4	318	10–0
32		130–133	4–8			319	10–1
33							
34							
35							
36							

Appendix C

A Form for Evaluating ITPA Part Scores

In interpreting the scores obtained on the ITPA, it is necessary to look at more than isolated scores. The global scores (PLA, PLQ, mean scaled score, and so on) are of limited significance except for comparison with other children and, most particularly, as points of reference in interpreting the part scores and scores on individual subtests. It is necessary to look at the various scores (a) in relation to each other, (b) in relation to patterns of abilities such as scores clustering in each of the three dimensions of the test, and (c) in relation to real-life situations and scores obtained on other tests.

The accompanying Form for Evaluating ITPA Part Scores was devised to simplify looking at the comparative scores in each of the three dimensions of the test: the *channels* of communication, the *processes* of communication, and the *levels* of communication. The summary sheet of the record form was specifically set up to make this possible. By summing each of the four columns of the summary sheet onto the Form for Evaluating ITPA Part Scores, comparisons of part scores in the three dimensions are apparent. In addition, the four columns of the summary sheet represent a further breakdown into (a) auditory/vocal subtests at the representational level, (b) auditory/vocal subtests at the automatic level, (c) visual/motor subtests at the representational level, and (d) visual/motor subtests at the automatic level.

A further discussion of the meaning of various deficits may be found in Kirk and Kirk, 1971.

FORM FOR EVALUATING ITPA PART SCORES

Name: Date of test:
Birthdate: PLA:
CA: PLQ:
                                                            Mean SS:

DIRECTIONS: Sum columns 1, 2, 3, and 4 from the summary sheet of the
ITPA Record Form and record in appropriate spaces below.
Calculate vertically for channel scores, horizontally for
others.

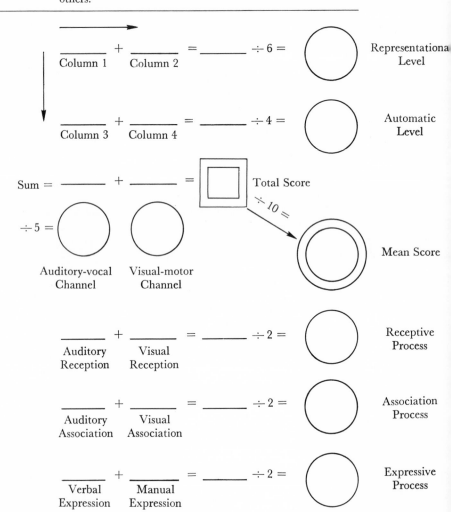

Appendix D

A Visual Aid for Learning to Administer
the Visual Sequential Memory Subtest

The following sequence of photographs depicts the step-by-step procedure in presenting the Visual Sequential Memory subtest. It is especially helpful in the early stages of learning to administer this subtest.

Note that the pictures are presented on one page while the corresponding verbal material is presented on the facing page and that the pictures are numbered to correspond with the appropriate words. It is recommended that as a potential examiner you should first study the directions and precautions presented in Chapter 3. Then study the sequence of pictures several times, reading the verbal material from the facing page and matching your actions to the words and pictures. After you have integrated the actions with the words, try going through the pictures with the facing page covered, supplying the verbal material yourself. You will find that after you have automated the demonstration items, the test items will fall into place automatically and you can give your attention to the details of recording, giving necessary second trials, sampling, and finding basals and ceilings.

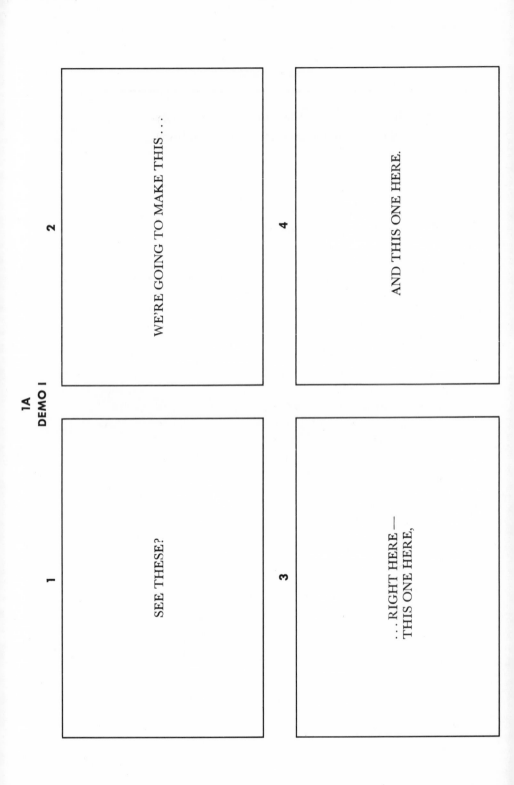

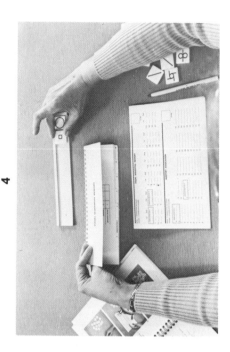

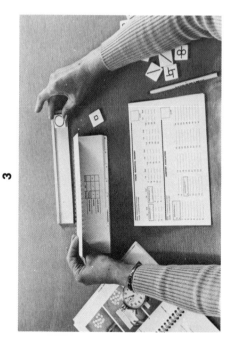

1B

1

2

3

4

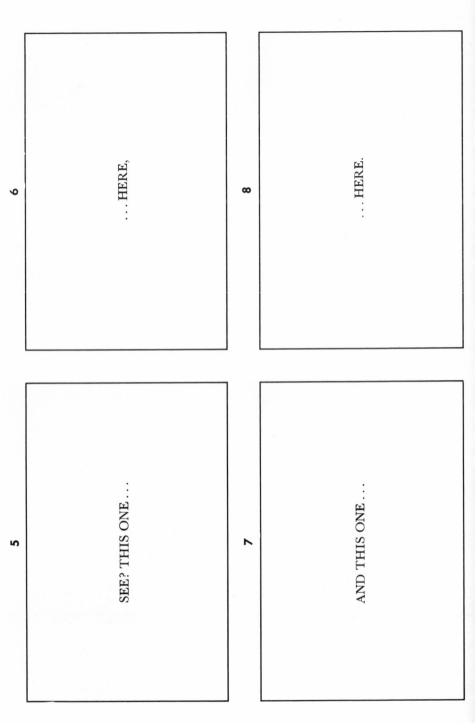

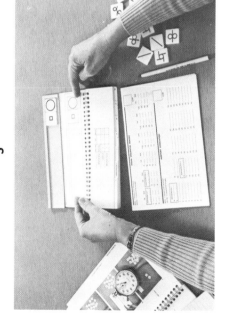

5

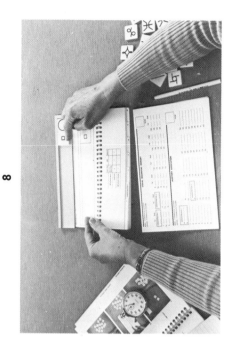

6

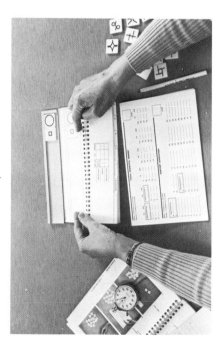

7

8

3A

9

. . . . . .

[Dump and shuffle.]

10

NOW LOOK AGAIN SO *YOU* CAN MAKE IT.
THIS ONE HERE,

11

AND THIS ONE HERE.

12

YOU DO IT;
MAKE IT HERE.

10

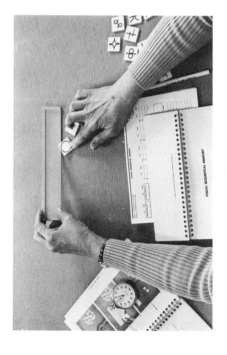

9

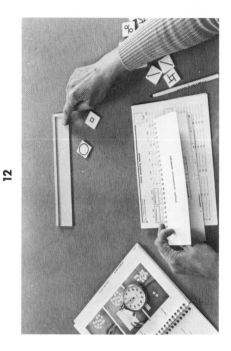

12

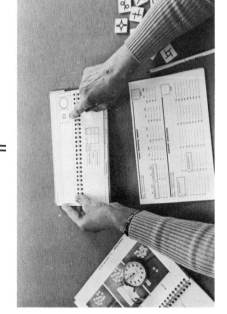

11

If response was correct:

13

YES, IT WAS LIKE THIS —
THIS ONE . . .

14

. . . HERE,

15

AND THIS ONE . . .

16

. . . HERE.

[Proceed to Item 2 (if sampling) or else to Item 1.]

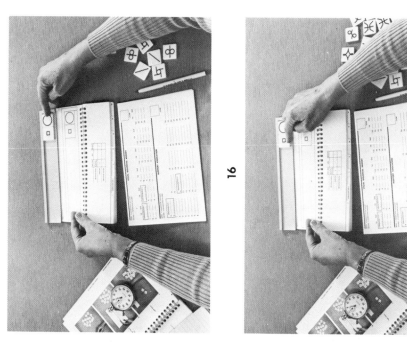

13

14

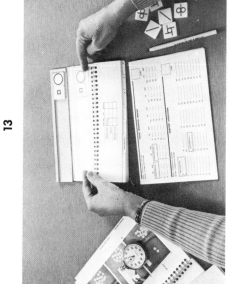

15

16

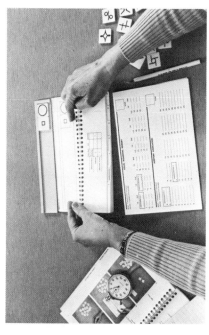

5A

If response was incorrect:

17

NO, IT WAS LIKE THIS —
THIS ONE . . .

18

. . . HERE,

19

AND THIS ONE . . .

20

. . . HERE.

[Repeat demonstration. When response is correct,
confirm (as on p. 4A) and proceed to Item 2
(if sampling) or else Item 1.]

18

20

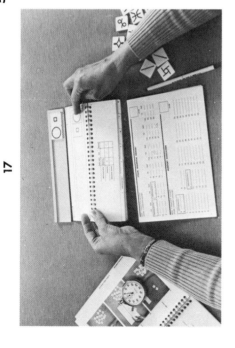

17

19

6A

Item 2 (if sampling)

21

. . . . .

[Add slash.]

22

. . . . .

[Dump and remove square.]

23

NOW LOOK AT THIS ONE —
THIS ONE HERE,

24

AND THIS ONE HERE.

[After 5 seconds:] YOU MAKE IT.
[If correct, go to Demo II, page 7A.]
[If incorrect, repeat as on page 8A.]

21

22

23

24

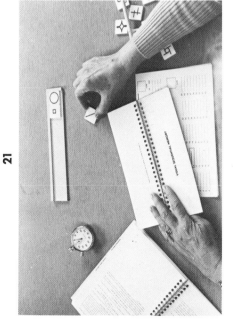

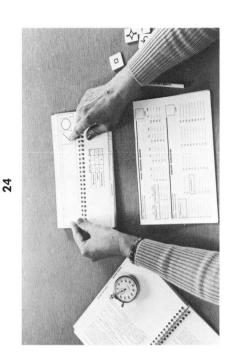

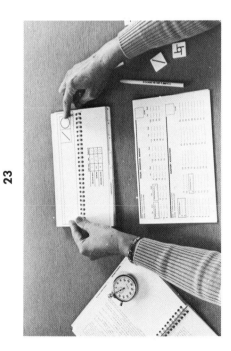

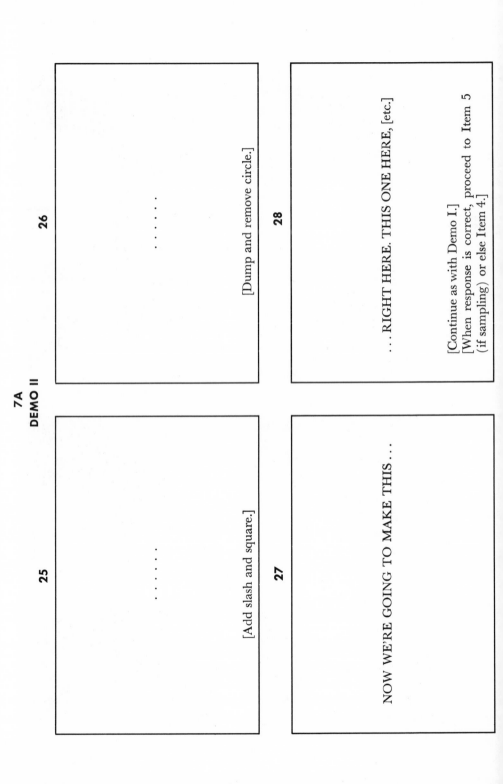

25

. . . . . .

[Add slash and square.]

26

. . . . .

[Dump and remove circle.]

27

NOW WE'RE GOING TO MAKE THIS . . .

28

. . . RIGHT HERE. THIS ONE HERE, [etc.]

[Continue as with Demo I.]
[When response is correct, proceed to Item 5
(if sampling) or else Item 4.]

25

26

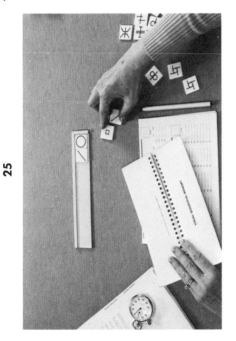

27

28

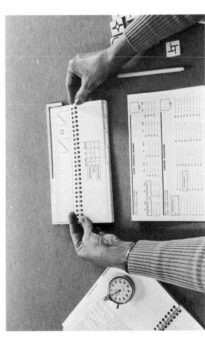

[If Item 2 (page 6) was incorrect:]

29

NOT QUITE,

[Dump and shuffle.]

30

LOOK AGAIN. THIS ONE HERE,

31

AND THIS ONE HERE.

[Begin 5 seconds.]

32

YOU MAKE IT.

[Regardless of success or failure on this trial, proceed to Item 1 since first trial was incorrect.]

29

30

31

32

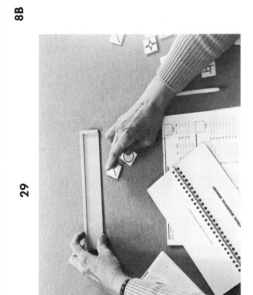

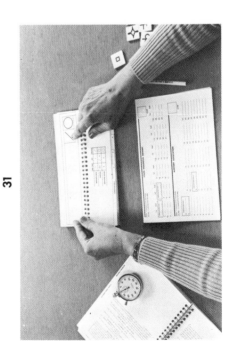

References

Button, L., Boland, S. K., and Todd, J. C. 1973. *ITPA bibliography for teachers of the learning disabled.* Greeley, Colo.: University of Northern Colorado, Rocky Mountain Special Education Instructional Materials Center.

Huizinga, R. J. 1973. The relationship of the ITPA to the Stanford-Binet Form L-M and the WISC. *Journal of Learning Disabilities.* 6 (7): 451–56.

Karnes, M. B. 1972. *GOAL: Language development.* Springfield, Mass.: Milton Bradley Co.

Kirk, S. A. 1972. Ethnic differences in psycholinguistic abilities. *Exceptional Children.* 39 (2): 112–19.

————, and Kirk, W. D. 1971. *Psycholinguistic learning disabilities: Diagnosis and remediation.* Urbana: University of Illinois Press.

————, McCarthy, J. J., and Kirk, W. D. 1968. *Examiner's manual, Illinois Test of Psycholinguistic Abilities.* Urbana: University of Illinois Press.

Kirk, W. D., and Kirk, S. A. 1969. *Film demonstration of the revised Illinois Test of Psycholinguistic Abilities.* Urbana: University of Illinois Press.

Minskoff, E., Wiseman, D., and Minskoff, J. G. 1973. *MWM language development program.* Ridgefield, N.J.: Educational Performance Associates.

Paraskevopoulos, J. N., and Kirk, S. A. 1969. *The development and psychometric characteristics of the revised Illinois Test of Psycholinguistic Abilities.* Urbana: University of Illinois Press.

Index

Age scores, 71–73, 82–83

American Psychological Association, 2

Auditory Association subtest: handling of negations, 10, 88; recording of, 12; scoring, 13

Auditory Closure subtest: one repetition only, 10, 88; use of tape recorder, 71

Auditory Reception subtest: basal requirement of, 8; reaching ceiling, 9; recording of, 12; use of alone, 70; questions about, 74

Auditory Sequential Memory subtest: use of Item 3 as Demo, 8; obtaining basal, 9; rate of presentation, 10–11; recording of, 12; use of tape recorder, 71; questions about, 71, 79

Auditory/vocal subtests, 95

Automatic level. See Levels of communication

Basals: precautions regarding, 8–9, 79–80, 87; scoring of failures below, 74, 75

Binet. See Stanford-Binet Intelligence Scale

Blacks, performance of, 82

Ceilings: precautions regarding, 9, 88; successes above, 74; in Visual Sequential Memory subtest, 80

Channels of communication, 95

Chronological age, 84

Composite PLA, 82, 84–85, 95

Creditable responses, in Verbal Expression, 32, 34–35

Demonstration items: where to begin testing, 7, 71; Demo II in Visual Association, 7–8; precautions regarding, 7–8, 87; in Visual Sequential Memory, 18–23, 79–80; in Sound Blending, 68, 81; Demo I instead of Demo II, 71

Dimensions of the ITPA, 95

"Don't know" answers, 9, 74

Efficiency, 2, 6–7, 87

Experimental Edition of the ITPA, 1, 78

Film Demonstration of the Revised ITPA, 17

Global scores, 95. *See also* Composite PLA, PLA, PLQ

Grammatic Closure subtest: use of second trial, 10, 63–65, 88; scoring, 13; care of materials, 14; use of alone, 70; use of tape recorder, 71; questions about, 78–79

Huizinga, Raleigh J., 84

Indians, performance of, 82

Interrogative responses, 36, 43

Intraindividual differences, 2, 81, 82. *See also* Scores

Invalidated tests, 71

IQ: ITPA as estimate of, 2, 84

Karnes, Merle B., 85

Kirk, Samuel A., 17, 70, 82, 83, 84, 85, 95

117